THERE IS A SOLUTION TO YOUR MONEY PROBLEMS

DALE E. GALLOWAY

G/L
REGAL
BOOKS™

A Division of G/L Publications
Glendale, California, U.S.A.

Additional Books in Print by the Author:
  Dream a New Dream, (Wheaton, Illinois:
  Tyndale Publishers, 1975).
  You Can Win with Love, (Irvine, California:
  Harvest House Publishers, 1976).
  We're Making Our Home a Happy Place,
  (Wheaton, Illinois: Tyndale Publishers, 1976)

Scriptures quoted in this publication are
from the following versions:
TLB, The Living Bible, Paraphrased (Wheaton: Tyndale
House, Publishers, 1971). Used by permission.
RSV, Revised Standard Version of the Bible, copyrighted
1946 and 1952 by the Division of Christian Education
of the NCCC in the U.S.A., and used by permission.
Phillips, The New Testament in Modern English, copyright
J.B. Phillips 1958. Used by permission of the
Macmillan Company.
NASB, New American Standard Bible. © The Lockman
Foundation, 1971. Used by permission.
TEV, Good News Bible, The Bible in Today's English
Version. Old Testament copyright © American Bible
Society 1966. New Testament copyright © American Bible
Society 1966, 1971, 1976. Used by permission.
KJV Authorized King James Version.

Published by
Regal Books Division, G/L Publications
Glendale, California 91209, U.S.A.
Printed in U.S.A.

Library of Congress Catalog Card No. 75-23518
ISBN 0-8307-0401-9

I dedicate this book
to my beloved father,
Dr. Harvey S. Galloway,
who was my example of
many of the principles
I share with you in this book.

To him the Lord has already
spoken these most appropriate
words, "Well done, thou good
and faithful servant."

CONTENTS

1
HELP! MONEY PROBLEMS GALORE

When I returned to my office one Wednesday afternoon there was an urgent message awaiting me from my wife, Margi. As I read the words they shocked me. Our fellow New Hope Church member, 25-year-old Vince Boylan, had just been told he had leukemia and was entering St. Vincent's Hospital for immediate treatment.

For the rest of the afternoon this puncturing reality kept stabbing me as I imagined how Vince and his wife, Cheryle, must be feeling. Not understanding why, I repeatedly cried out to God, "Father, you know they haven't been Christians very long, but this is just too much—it's too heavy. Besides, what do you expect me to say to them?"

7

After holding a wrestling match inside myself, wanting to see my friend and yet not knowing what to say, Margi and I got into our car and headed for St. Vincent's Hospital. I hadn't yet found the words to tell Margi that I had concluded within myself that I didn't have any answers and would just sit down and cry with my hurting friends, the Boylans.

As we entered the stricken patient's room, we were immediately met by an unexpected smile on Vince's face, and from that moment until we left, the patient and his devoted wife, Cheryle, cheered up me and my wife. Face to face with the most depressing of difficulties, these new Christians' positive faith came charging through.

Strength Beyond Yourself

In this book you are going to find the positive strength beyond yourself to get on top of even the most depressing of situations. I am going to show you that there is no money problem that, with the attitude and principles God wants to give you, you cannot overcome.

Feeling keen brotherly love for Vince while visiting him on the second day, I approached him about how his church family might help him financially. He shared with me that Cheryle and he had already made the financial decision that, to cut down on living expenses, they would give up their apartment and she and their little girl, Chrissi, would move in with her folks. I was glad to tell my friend that he would not have to worry at all about how to move the furniture because his Christian brothers would supply the helping hands.

It was then that a warm, happy smile broke out across my ailing friend's face. With a sense of glowing pride, he told me how they had made the decision one year before to practice the money principles I had taught them, and that others in our church were already enjoying the benefits from this. Previously they had been burdened down with a staggering debt load, but because they had decided to take action and had persistently followed through, now that they were facing physical and economical crises, they were debt-free.

That afternoon, as I climbed into my Mustang and headed back to the office, I thanked God that I had shared more than a year ago with these friends what God had taught me about solving money problems. Then, a short month later, as I preached at the funeral of my departed friend, Vince, and looked into the eyes of the young widow left with a small child, I said a double thanks that she didn't have those old depressing debts to worry about.

The Time to Solve Your Money Problems Is Now!

How to solve your money problems is what you are going to learn in this book.

At one of our creative Bible fellowship groups, I asked the participants to list all the problems related to the handling of money. This is the revealing list they came up with:

Emotional depression
Negative reactions
Physical illness
Undue stress
Mental breakdowns
Loose living from having too much money
Mixed-up priorities and values
Discontent and dissatisfaction

Low self-image
Envy of what other people have
Jealousy
Worry
Marital conflict
Loss of desire to dream of bigger things
Loss of energy and enthusiasm
Loss of values
Spiritual defeat and loss of joy.

Having completed this long list of problems connected either directly or indirectly with money, the group made this astounding deduction: "There is no end to the number of heartbreaking and relationship-breaking problems arising out of money matters." Whether or not an individual accepts the responsibility for handling his money, how he handles it or fails to handle it does matter.

What an emotional toll money problems and poor money management are taking on the American family! For more than 16 years as a marriage counselor I have seen too many families literally torn apart over money matters. It would be conservative to say that 75 percent of all families suffer severely from stress and tension caused by unnecessary money problems:

So much marriage tension
So much marriage discord
So much marriage misunderstanding
So much marriage anger
So much marriage brokenness

So many of these problems could be stopped quickly, by reading and practicing the practical truths contained in this book. If you are a single person, this book can help you:

Overcome money anxiety

Have more instead of less

Build a good and prosperous life for yourself

Let's be honest—just about everyone has money problems. I've observed that some people stand up straight and face their money problems. They learn from their past mistakes; they open up to God's better way for them to manage; and sooner or later they do solve their money problems.

But a throng of people in our society, to their own detriment, refuse to face reality about the cause of their money problems. Once in a while in their more sober moments they allow themselves to think about it for a fleeting moment. But such serious thinking is swiftly stopped by the false conclusion that the problems will somehow solve themselves.

Some even resort to escaping painful money truths by doubling their efforts to spend more money that they don't have, which of course adds fuel to the fire and gets them into still heavier money problems. Such failure to face reality will never bring you the good life you really want. This book is not only for all those who want the good life, but it is for those who have the courage to face some financial realities of life.

Gary was all excited as he announced to the congregation that he had just made his last debt payment. I remember the day Gary came to see me. For the first time he faced the seriousness of his money problems—harassment by bill collectors, tension in his marriage, and damaged self-image because there was never enough money to provide for his family as he thought a man should. Now, less then 18 months later, the depressing debts were all paid—time for a celebration!

Two months after paying off the debts, Gary took his whole family on the happy experience of a two-week vacation with the sheer joy of paying for everything in cash as they went. How wonderful to enjoy a paid-for vacation without the hangover of depressing money problems!

There Is a Solution to Your Money Problems

You do not have any money problem that is so great that it cannot be overcome. Whatever else, keep this one fact in mind: For every problem there is a solution. You see, there is the law of opposites; for every night there is a day, for every valley there is a mountain, for every problem there is a solution. Whatever you do, don't ever, ever give up. As the Scriptures put it, "I have the strength to face all conditions by the power that Christ gives me" (Phil. 4:13, *TEV*).

If you, like most people, have money problems, I congratulate you. I congratulate you first of all because dead people don't have problems. If you have problems that means you are alive. One of the neat things that God has been teaching me is that in every perplexing problem there is a striking opportunity.

One of our young mothers, who has shown tremendous growth spiritually, told me that last winter when they were having not just *one* money problem and not just *two* money problems but *compounded* money problems, she learned some of the most significant practical spiritual lessons. The first thing she learned was to make God her source, to depend upon Him. Then she learned something about true riches and what was of lasting value. Then God taught her that when she and her husband put Him first, He would supply their daily needs.

Exuberantly she testified that out of depressing money problems God taught them lessons from their mistakes and mismanagement and showed them how to practice biblical principles of money management.

Your money problems are great opportunities for you to learn, to advance, to overcome—not only for your own good, but for your family's well-being and for the glory of God.

In the pages to come, we are going to learn how to develop the right attitude toward money, how to practice sound biblical principles of finance, and how to sow the seeds of faith and thereby receive a multiplied return of unlimited supply. It's going to be exciting, and I welcome you aboard one of the most important journeys of your life!

2
WHY WORRY AND FRET OVER MONEY?

"He—is—going—to—leave—me," the emotionally wrought young wife squeaked out between sobs. Everyone thought Larry and Sandra made such a handsome couple together. I had been at their wedding two years before, and I saw by the way they looked at each other how deeply in love they were. Now, only two years later, I invited Sandra to sit down and tell me all about it. For what seemed like forever she chattered on and on about a lot of things which didn't mean very much.

Then with a great deal of reluctance she blurted out, "I am frigid." Shrugging her shoulders in a gesture of hopelessness she said, "It's just no use—I can't respond to Larry, and he says if I don't start responding soon he is going to leave me." From Sandra's words it was apparent that in spite of this young couple's love for each other they were experiencing painful hurt and misunderstanding in an intimate area of relationship in which God intended for them to experience great joy.

But more often than not what we *think* is our problem is merely the tip of the iceberg. As Sandra talked to me further, the root cause of her inability to respond to her husband revealed itself. Do you have any idea what it was that had caused this lady to become so uptight inside that she became unresponsive to her husband? The root cause of all this trouble was that Sandra was worried sick over unpaid bills. Worry over money robbed her of peace of mind, then negative worry so hindered the functioning of her mind that anything positive (like responding to her husband) became unobtainable. And now, in its more advanced stages of destruction, worry over money was threatening to split the sheets between two people who really loved each other.

One man was confessing for a great many of us when he said, "I am just a worry boy, and I know it. The inner tension is seldom relaxed from morning to night, and the strain of it is terrible. The word *money* by itself is enough to set me off on a worrying spree."

Worried about money? If so, you are not alone. Just yesterday over a cup of coffee with a friend (a professional counselor), I was told that he was becoming all uptight over money, or rather the lack of money. Interestingly, both the haves and the have-nots worry over money. Those who have it worry themselves to death over how to keep it, while those who don't have it worry themselves into an early grave over how they can get it! *Let's admit it—we all know what it is to go on a worrying spree over money.*

A professor of psychology at California State University claims that 90 percent of all illness is caused by money worries. A recent woman's magazine featured a survey which showed that 75 percent of all worries are about money. You know it and I know it—we don't need a survey to tell us that an overwhelming majority of all our worries are either directly or indirectly related to money problems. You have a good mind and are an intelligent person, so why, I ask you, should you worry and fret over money?

These things you need to know: Worrying over money will not change anything; it will not add one day to your life; it will not pay one bill; it will not solve your money problems; it will not change anything; it will not make you any happier, but instead will make you miserable. So I ask you again, why should you worry and fret over money?

Why Worry and Fret over Money?

Far too many times we are robbed of good health because we allow the negative emotion of worry to impair the function of our control center. Worry instantly disturbs one's peace of mind. Someone has described fret as spiritual heartburn. Fretting is like having your car in the mud, stepping on the gas, spinning your wheels, and all the time going nowhere. There is nothing that wears a person out more emotionally than fretting and worrying over money problems.

The word *worry* is derived from an old Anglo-Saxon word meaning to strangle or to choke. If someone were to place his fingers around your throat and press with full strength, cutting off your vital air supply, he would be doing to you what you do to yourself emotionally when you worry. You block off your own flow of vital psychic energy. Worry frustrates your best functioning.

Have you ever heard anyone say, "I'm almost sick with worry," and then add with a laugh, "But I guess worry never really makes anyone ill"? But that is where the person is wrong. Worry *can* make you ill. Worry makes millions ill every day.

I hadn't the slightest idea that my friend Sam had

been feeling ill for several months, so it came as a shock when his wife phoned me and, in a pleading voice, begged me to go see him immediately at the local hospital. I had just talked to him on the phone the day before and he had not given me any inkling of being sick.

I was unprepared for the disturbed state of mind in which I found my friend when I visited him at the hospital. When I saw beads of perspiration on his forehead and looked into his anxiety-filled eyes, I knew something was terrifying him to death.

When I asked Sam if he would like to talk about what was troubling him, an upsetting story came tumbling out. He was sure he had cancer, and he had been living with this dreadful fear for months. I asked if a doctor had told him that he had cancer. He said, "No, I hadn't even seen a doctor until yesterday." But because he was a heavy smoker, and because of some symptoms he was feeling, Sam just knew he was destined to die of lung cancer in a few days. He told me that he was so convinced of his impending death that a few days before, while fishing, he had come ever so close to intentionally drowning himself.

Early the next morning, following my visit with Sam, the doctors came in and told him, "We have taken all the tests and we find you to be in perfect health; you may go home now." He had built it all up in his imagination! Sam had made himself sick with worry.

A conversation with Sam a few days later revealed that his problems started six months before his hospital experience, when he was worrying over money. He had worried himself into feeling ill, and the more miserable he felt the more he worried, not only about his money but also about his health, until he became convinced that he had cancer. Worrying over money caused my friend to come within an inch of death itself, to say nothing of the months of suffering and mental anguish.

Worry depletes and destroys the body. Anxiety destroys people's minds. It blurs thinking processes and distorts reason. Worry spoils the disposition. It makes you irritable, gloomy, impatient, and bad-tempered. Worries drain off our energies. One remedy for excessive worry is a clear understanding of just how much damage it does to us. Worry can curdle your expression, ruin your complexion, cause crippling arthritis, rob you of happiness.

Worry is not incurable. There is a remedy for the sickness. People say, "Oh, I know it's silly to worry, but I just can't help it." How wrong they are! In the first place, it's not *silly* but *stupid* to worry. Second, we *can* help it! We must stop excusing ourselves. If worry had been incurable, Jesus would not have said, "Do not be anxious" (Matt. 6:25, *RSV*). Oswald Chambers says, "All our fret and worry is caused by calculating without God."

How to Stop Worrying over Money

Take the first step to win over worry: tell yourself that *worry is useless.* "Will all your worries add a single moment to your life?" asked Jesus (Matt. 6:27, *TLB*). When you worry, it changes nothing, gets you absolutely nowhere, accomplishes zero. The truth is that worry always hurts you.

One woman has a successful method of combating worry. Each time she feels herself getting stirred up about something, she says, "The tendency to brood and fret never solved any problem yet. Worry is a rocking

19

chair that never takes me anywhere." Decide now that you will *never worry about anything that is not in your power to change.*

Choose to live one day at a time. Refuse to carry problems and anxieties from one day into the next. When a day is over, drop the curtain. Put it in God's hands. You can't do anything to alter that day. That day is done. Reach forth to the new day. Believe it: Today is the first day of the rest of your life.

Stop worrying about the future. Who holds the future? God does! I belong to Someone who has charge of the future. It does me no good to fret and stew over something that will never happen. And if it does happen, His strength will be given to me at that time—not before that time. When I stew ahead of time, I do it all on my own. Jesus said, "So don't be anxious about tomorrow. God will take care of your tomorrow too. Live one day at a time" (Matt. 6:34, *TLB*). Security comes from a spiritual state of mind, not from a changing world.

God Is Concerned About Your Material Needs

God is where the need is. Wherever there is a need, that's where you can look for God and find Him every time. One of my favorite stories is recorded in all four of the Gospels. It is the feeding of the 5,000 —5,000 people without food and in desperate need. The disciples suggested sending them away to buy bread, but Jesus said, "If I do, then they will faint by the wayside." Jesus became immediately concerned about bread, and bread here represents the totality of man's needs.

God is concerned about daily bread. In our Lord's Prayer Jesus teaches us to pray, "Give us this day our daily bread." So many would have us think of religion

20

as something far-off, pie-in-the-sky, so to speak. Well, I want to tell you that God is concerned about the bread for your physical needs here and now. I believe that God is interested in the energy crisis; that He is deeply concerned about inflation that eats away at all of our incomes; that He is intensely interested in you if you are unemployed or in need of a better job.

Last Wednesday night a runaway girl, two days without food and out of money, phoned for help. I believe that as she cried out for help, God directed her to call one of our families, and for them in turn to phone me. In responding, one of our lay pastors and I had the joy of being used of God to help this young girl. We paid for her room, took her to a restaurant, and received joy from watching her enjoy eating her first meal in two days. Then the next day we put her on a bus to return back home. Yes, God is interested in all of our needs.

An imaginary story is told of two birds flying through the morning breeze. Jaybird says to Robin, "Look down there at all those humans fretting themselves to death." To this, Robin replies, "You know, they must not have a heavenly Father like you and me."

Jesus said, "Look at the birds! They don't worry about what to eat—they don't need to sow or reap or store up food—for your heavenly Father feeds them. And you are far more valuable to him than they are" (Matt. 6:26, *TLB*).

Look to Your Heavenly Father

What is your need? Is your need for food? Do you have some outstanding pressing obligations that are due? Are you in need of a better income? Do you find yourself in need of a job? People have many needs;

everyone has some need. What is your need? Whatever your need, this promise is for you: "God shall supply all your need according to his riches in glory by Christ Jesus" (Phil. 4:19, *KJV*).

God wants to supply your need! April 24, 1974, was an unforgettable day in the life of the Galloways. For me it was an experience unequaled in warmth, beauty, and breathtaking excitement to be holding my wife Margi's hand as our daughter Ann entered our world. What extra joy Ann has added to our home! You have heard it said that everything costs plenty these days, and having a baby is no exception.

We had health insurance, but it was $500 short of paying our bill. Due to some other unexpected emergencies, we only had $55 to pay toward the remaining balance. So I made an agreement with the hospital that within 90 days we would pay the remaining $445. All too swiftly the days came and went, and suddenly it was the eighty-ninth day, one day before the money was due. With the extra expenses of a new baby, we had not been able to squeeze out 10 extra dollars, let alone $445. What would we do?

On that Thursday morning during our family prayer, as Margi prayed, she reminded the Lord that we had endeavored to put Him first in everything. We had applied Matthew 6:33, "Seek ye first the kingdom of God, and his righteousness; and all these things shall be added unto you." Then she boldly concluded, "We have done our part Lord; now we are waiting to see what you are going to do to provide for our need." As I left for the office Margi reiterated her unquestioning belief that God was going to take care of us. Well, I believed it, but I still thought I had better think of something quick.

Throughout that Thursday, at various times, I would think about this pressing need and would breathe a prayer to my heavenly Father, asking Him to supply our need or to show me just what I should do.

That evening I received a phone call from a realtor. He represented a client who wanted to buy a sewer easement along the east side of our home property; the client needed the easement to develop some land behind our property. An appointment was set for the next morning.

With great anticipation Margi and I awaited Friday morning to see just what God was going to do to meet our pressing need. The young man arrived promptly at my office, introduced himself, sat down, and told me his client would give me $250 if I would simply sign on a sheet of paper. I silently asked in prayer, "What should I do, Lord? This is only half the money I need." Then I took a deep breath and said, "I will be happy to sign for $500." He said he would check with his client and get back to me.

After he left, I could't help wondering if I had blown it by asking for too much. Exactly 20 minutes later my phone rang. It was the realtor and he said, "My client will pay you the $500 immediately if you will sign now." I could hardly wait to hang up the phone so I could share the good news with Margi. Within two days we had the $500. We paid the hospital $445, gave our $50 tithe to God, and had five dollars left over for a family treat. Together we thanked the Lord for supplying our every need.

There is no limit to what God wants to give you. Not only does God want to supply your needs, but He wants to give you so much more. Many are familiar with God's promises to supply their daily needs. But did you know that He wants to give you *the desires of your heart?*

For a mind-expanding exercise, fix your thoughts upon these power-packed promises:

> Psalm 37:4: "Delight thyself also in the Lord; and he shall give thee the desires of thine heart" (*KJV*). Think of it! God wants to give you the desires of your heart.

> Mark 11:24: "Listen to me! You can pray for *anything*, and *if you believe, you have it;* it's yours!" (*TLB*). What a promise!

God doesn't want you to just squeak by, barely making ends meet. God wants to give to you out of His abundance, to give you more, so much more! Like a father gives good gifts to his children, God delights in giving the very best to you, His children. Jesus said, "And if you hardhearted, sinful men know how to give good gifts to your children, won't your Father in heaven even more certainly give good gifts to those who ask him for them?" (Matt. 7:11, *TLB*).

The Key Principle—Make God Your Source

Shortages! Gas shortages, energy shortages, paper shortages, food shortages, money shortages. All shortages are man-made. They are the result of sin and slothfulness, abuse and misuse, greed and games. But there are no shortages with God! His riches are without limit, above and beyond anything our minds can fathom.

There are no limits to God's prosperity.

God owns all the real estate. "The earth is the Lord's, and the fulness thereof; the world, and they that dwell therein" (Ps. 24:1, *KJV*).

God owns all the cattle. "For every beast of the forest

is mine, and the cattle upon a thousand hills" (Ps. 50:10, *KJV*).

God owns the financial world. "The silver is mine, and the gold is mine, saith the Lord of hosts" (Hag. 2:8, *KJV*).

There are no shortages with God, only surpluses. Unbelievable, but true! God wants you to be His partner in prosperity. Jesus brought us this word: "I am come that they might have life, and that they might have it more abundantly" (John 10:10, *KJV*). The Scriptures teach us that we are "heirs of God, and joint-heirs with Christ" (Rom. 8:17, *KJV*). Think of it—you are to be a joint-heir with Jesus Christ to all the treasures of the heavenly empire!

During the summer months preceding my founding of the New Hope Community Church in October of 1972, I learned a very important lesson. Preparing to launch my lifetime dream, I selected a list of 10 people and proceeded to try to solicit their financial support. I went to see each prospective supporter and shared in great detail my dream to build Oregon's first drive-in, walk-in church for the unchurched thousands.

After painting the beautiful picture of my dream, I challenged each of them to become my partner in this God-given dream. When I had finished sharing with all 10 of my sources, I had exactly zero amount of money and, boy, was I discouraged! I felt I was beaten before I even got started. I even made the added mistake of beginning to blame some of these good people for their failure to respond to my vision for New Hope. I was looking to these people to be my source of financial supply. What a transforming day it was when I discovered that I needed to make *God* my source!

25

Make God your source and anything is possible. Without any financial support, but with a big God as my sole source, I rented the 82nd Drive-In Theater and set the date for our opening service. During these past four years God has supplied every financial need and multiplied His expanding ministry hundreds of times. In partnership with God you, too, can achieve great things.

God has never let me down. I have found that God is too good to do bad, too wise to make a mistake, too strong to fail, too interested to ignore us.

It is absolutely unbelievable what God can and will do in your life and through your life as you make Him your source. You can see your dreams fulfilled, your projects completed, and great things accomplished. Your key to unlimited prosperity is to be found in this tremendous Bible verse: "But seek ye first the kingdom of God and his righteousness; and all these things shall be added unto you" (Matt. 6:33, *KJV*).

I hate to admit it, but sometimes I still forget who my Source is, and as a result I begin again to worry and fret over money. Distressing worry becomes my heartburn every time I begin to calculate without God. One of my big heroes of the Bible is Peter. I particularly love the story where he gets out on the water and by faith begins walking on the water to Jesus. Look at him, walking on water! Whoops! Down he goes. Peter took his eyes off the power Source, Jesus! Every time I take my eyes off Jesus and stop trusting, it is disastrous.

It is true—you should not trust what the devil says, because he is a liar; your own efforts, because they are never enough; in the government, because they are already overextended in their credit; in some people, because they will let you down; in earthly riches, because it will all pass away. *But why should you worry and fret when you can trust in the Lord?*

Why Worry and Fret When You Can Commit?

You don't have to cook yourself into a stew over money problems. By practicing the principle I am now going to share with you, you will be saved from all the anxiety people suffer because they emotionally focus on money or the lack of it.

Barbara was a 29-year-old single girl who had a good-paying job. But because she knew very little about managing money, she found herself getting behind in her current obligations. Soon she was worrying and fretting over money to such an extent that she was ill a lot of the time and didn't feel like going to work. Time lost at work resulted in losses in income, which only worsened her situation.

By the time Barbara came to see me, she had cooked herself into a thickening mental stew. Worry can really make a person suffer, and Barbara was suffering.

After Barbara talked for quite awhile I said, "Barbara, you have a dual problem. You have an attitude problem and an action problem. You have permitted your attitude to become negative with worry over money. Also, you need to learn the basic principles about how to manage your money. I'll be very glad to teach you these money management principles that have helped so many people. But first, let's deal with your negative attitude of worry over money."

Opening my Bible to Psalm 37, I handed it to Barbara and asked her to read. After she had read the first six verses out loud I said, "Barbara, what are the very first two words in that psalm?" She looked at the passage and

27

answered, "Fret not" (Ps. 37:1, *KJV*). I then asked Barbara to read verse five. These are the words that she read out loud: "Commit everything you do to the Lord. Trust him to help you do it and he will" (Ps. 37:5, *TLB*). I then pointed out to Barbara that the very first word was an action word that tells us exactly what we are to do with all worrying and fretting. We are to *commit.*

I said to Barbara, "Why should you worry and fret over money when you can commit all your money problems to God? Barbara, there is something I want you to do for me, okay?" She nodded; I guess at this point she would do almost anything to get help.

I continued, "Barbara, cup your hands together. Now I want you to take every money problem that you are worried about and put it right there in the cup. Do it now! Your unpaid bills, your fear about tomorrow, your fear that your health is not going to hold out." Barbara began to cry.

"Barbara, take your cup with all your worries and give it to God. Now turn your hands over and say these words after me. 'Here it is, Lord, it is too heavy for me to carry any longer.' Now, Barbara, spread your fingers apart and release the worry. *Let go and let God have it.*"

As Barbara finished this spiritual exercise in releasing prayer, her face lighted up with a smile that I hadn't seen in months. Faith had replaced fretting!

This very day accept God's solution to rid you of worrying and fretting over money.

"Don't worry about anything; instead, pray about everything; tell God your needs and don't forget to thank him for his answers. If you do this you will experience God's peace, which is far more wonderful than the human mind can understand" (Phil. 4:6,7 *TLB*).

Why Worry and Fret When You Can Take Action?

As we have been learning in this chapter, it is wrong for us to worry and fret over money. But let's acknowledge here and now that it is a good thing to be *concerned* about money. Until we become concerned, we won't do anything to make our situation better. While it is true that money is not worth *worrying* about, it does need your *concern*.

Believe it—you and God together can turn your money situation around. You can learn valuable lessons from your money failures and move ahead to successfully manage your money. I have seen scores of people in financial straits who took new courage, received insights, learned lessons, dug in, and with unyielding determination changed their unstable financial picture into a stable one.

Some years ago I read this story in one of Dr. Norman Vincent Peale's published sermons:

A debt doctor, better known as a bill collector, shared this true experience: "I was called in to collect from a young couple not too long ago. They were terribly distraught; they didn't know what to do. They had bought too much, too fast—a car, a television, furniture, and so on.

"They were hurling recriminations at one another. 'It's all your fault!' 'It isn't! It's your fault!' And their kids were cowering in the corner. So I said, 'Now let's all sit down here and have a little talk. Where are the bills?' 'Bills?' they exclaimed. 'We've got nothing but bills!'

" 'Well, let me see them,' I said. So they

29

brought the bills out. 'Well, you owe so much here. Put that down. I see you owe so-and-so this amount. Put that down. And you owe this fellow here so much. Put that down. I see you got a second and third bill from this one; okay, we'll put it right down here.

" 'Now that we've got them all in piles, let's add up how much we owe this one, that one, and the other one, and then let's add up the total.' After getting the total I said, 'Now, you know that isn't so terribly much when you think about it. Anybody with intelligence could overcome that after a while just by hard work and planning.' 'But,' they said, 'We haven't got any money.'

"So I said, 'This is what we'll do. We'll tell the owner of Smith Radio and TV that you'll pay him a dollar a week, but he can count on it every week on Monday—one dollar. And Mr. Jones of the garage, give him a dollar a week.' 'Why,' they said, 'they wouldn't take that small amount of money.'

"I said, 'Don't you know that a creditor who has already written off the account would be glad to get a dollar if he was sure he was going to get it? I'll write to all these people, and I'll venture there won't be a single one that will turn down this plan.' And then I prayed with these people to let God take over in their finances, because now the confusion had been taken away and with it the panic. They now had a plan.

"And they paid every one of those bills. I

told them to buy nothing in the meantime and they didn't. They solved their financial problem. They learned what was the right thing to do. They also discovered that God would help them, and the spirit of truth came into the matter."[1]

When I was a boy my father used to say to me, "Son, God expects you to do your very best in life on whatever project you are working. Then He wants you to trust Him as if it all depended upon Him. Do this and you'll have a successful life."

God expects us to work at solving our money problems, to do everything we can do to manage well what He has given us. God will not do for any one of us what we are capable in body and mind of doing for ourself. He is too wise for that. Our heavenly Father wants what is best for us; He wants it too much to allow us to be lazy, slothful, or irresponsible. But when you have done your part, you can count on Him doing more than His part.

RIGHT ATTITUDE AND RIGHT ACTIONS
COMBINED WITH GOD'S HELP
ARE GOING TO RESULT IN
YOUR GAINING ALTITUDE FINANCIALLY.

Footnote

1. Norman Vincent Peale (Pawling, N.Y.: Foundation for Christian Living). Used by Permission.

3

THE FIRST STEP TO SOLVING YOUR MONEY PROBLEMS

When we have personal money problems, who is responsible for our difficulties? Those who rip us off? The government? Runaway inflation? Rising oil prices? Banks and creditors. Our employers? Changing economic conditions?

Who is to blame when we are squeezed financially? One young man told me that he felt like a defenseless block caught in a vise, unable to stop the monster from squeezing him tighter and tighter. We all know that outside forces beyond our individual control are squeezing us financially. But which one of us can afford the high price, physically and psychologically, of getting ourselves into a negative cycle by playing the blame game? Playing the blame game is no way to find a solution; it only serves to fill one's mind with pollution.

Sue was noticeably nervous and apprehensive sitting in my office, while her husband, Ken, gave the "let me at him" appearance of a prizefighter just before stepping into the ring to devour another victim. For months I had been receiving bits and pieces that these friends were in deep financial trouble. As their pastor, I had been praying that they would face up to their money problems and come to see me for help.

In order to put Sue at ease, while at the same moment trying to cool her husband's aggressive anger, I said, "I congratulate you." Unbelieving Sue challenged, "You congratulate us for being head-over-heels in debt?" And Ken snapped, "You congratulate us for running way from bill collectors for two years?"

I explained, "I congratulate you for making the decision to come here today and face up to your money problems. For you I have tremendous hope!"

Now that I had their undivided attention, I seized the opportunity to explain the hard financial facts of life. "No one is going to manage your money for you. And dear friends, unless you make up your minds to become responsible for managing your money, you are going to continue to be in a mess financially."

Looking straight at Ken and Sue, I asked, "Aren't you tired of all these money problems?" Ken sneeringly reacted, "What a silly question; do you think we would be here if we didn't want help?"

Not to be sidetracked, I pressed on with these questions: "Are the two of you ready to start managing your money starting right now?" What a beautiful new beginning of better things to come as my two friends committed themselves to managing their money!

Friend, this is the one step no one can take for you,

like it or not. Ignore this decisive point, and, whatever else you do, your financial problems will neither dissolve nor decrease. If you are earnest about solving your money problems, and I believe you are, then take one giant step forward by deciding that, come what may, *you* are going to manage your money!

To fail to decide to manage your money—

Is to abuse and misuse what God gives you;

Is to open the door wide open for multiple money
   problems;

Is to be the slave of money instead of the
   master;

Is to settle for the lesser instead of claiming
   the greater.

In Luke 19, our Lord Jesus tells what has become a very familiar parable. The story is about a wealthy man who has great holdings and enormous assets. Preparing to be gone for a period of time, he divides up his assets among several of his servants to manage and care for in his absence. Upon his return, he calls in the servants and asks for a full accounting of how well they have done in managing what he has given them. One has excelled in his management and another has done quite well, but the third has completely failed to take the responsibility of being a manager.

The point that Jesus is making is this: Each of us is given the responsibility of something to manage. It is not how much we have been given that counts, but it is a matter of how well we manage what we have. Do a good job managing what you have, and you will be given more. "But it is always true that those who have, get more, and those who have little, soon lose even that" (Luke 19:26, *TLB*).

You Are Responsible to Manage Your Money

To be wise in managing your money is much more important than earning a large income. Money management must be a shared concern of each member of a family. There is no area of family relationships that demands more communication and cooperation than the area of finances. I remember hearing an old-timer tell about working a team of horses in the field, where getting the job accomplished depended upon the horses working together as a team. The old-timer said, "It was the horses that worked together that got the most done in a day." It is the family that *works together* that gets the greatest results in the area of financial management. What is good for all is good for you.

When God created male and female it was His divine plan that they might complement each other and together achieve marvelous things. God created male and female different from each other, yet both of supreme worth in His sight. Those who are pitting man and woman against each other in competition have done our society a disastrous disservice. God never meant for a man and a woman to be pitted against each other.

At the very core of good family finance is the need to understand and accept man's and woman's different God-given responsibilities and to work together in full cooperation.

What is the husband's responsibility? Any successful organization, whether a church, a school or a thriving business, must have a strong leader at the helm. It is the leader's job not only to care for immediate needs, but to do long-range planning. As financial leader in the home, the man should be *planning ahead.*

God calls all men to stand up to their God-given

36

responsibility. Show me a family that is floundering financially and in the majority of cases there will be no male leader at the helm. When the captain is constantly asleep below deck, the ship is going to get into serious trouble.

Unfortunately, for many families, some men hold to the mistaken notion that their job is only to *earn* the money. Wake up, family captain! To earn the money is not enough; the earning must be *managed!*

I believe it is biblical and psychologically right that a man should carry the bulk of the responsibility for facing unpaid bills, insufficient funds, and other problems which occur when money runs short. He will want to openly share with his wife about the needs, but he needs to spend time thinking about his financial problems and seeking solutions to them. For every problem there is a solution.

Through asserting strong leadership and taking responsibility for the overall management of finances, a man can save his wife from undue stress and strain. Often a man's lack of aggressive leadership in the area of finances creates a vacuum of worry and stress within his wife. A woman's greatest need is for security. Happy is the wife and blessed is the husband who through his financial leadership provides an atmosphere of security.

What is the wife's responsibility? Although the wife's financial responsibility is different from her husband's, it is of equal importance in the successful management of the family money. Her responsibilities are fourfold:

First, she is to be a sounding board for her husband, a person with whom he can openly share his plans and decisions in solving money problems and in reaching financial goals.

Second, she is to cooperate with her husband and thus create a spirit of harmony in the home.

Third, she is to make a dollar stretch in the money that is assigned to her.

Fourth, she is to share helpful suggestions with her husband.

Manage Your Money by Objectives

What are your financial objectives? Throughout your lifetime, do you want to keep on struggling to make ends meet? Or would you like to get on top of things? What is it that you want to achieve financially in your lifetime? In the next five years, what do you want to accomplish with your money? Do you have any financial plans for the next 12 months?

Multitudes of people are sinking financially simply because they have no financial blueprint. Would you contract with a builder who was known for not using blueprints to build you a new home? If you did, it would be like throwing your money away, and you are a whole lot smarter than that! And yet, many of us keep throwing our money away simply because we have no pattern or plan by which we manage our money.

Someone has said, "When you fail to plan, you are planning to fail." There is no area of life in which this is more true than in the area of finances. To plan is to predetermine your course of action. The only alternative to planning is to act without forethought. Instead of leaving your financial future to chance, it is far better to decide now where you want to go and to start planning how you are going to get there.

Decide where it is you want to go, and plan how you are going to arrive at your destination.

1. Take an honest look at where you are financially.
Phil and Bonnie, by their own admission, had been guilty of hiding their heads in the sand when it came to money matters.

For more than six months they had not even bothered to take the time to balance their checkbook and the results as you can imagine were a barrage of bounced checks. They had acquired the bad habit of stuffing unpaid bills in the desk drawer in the spare bedroom where they seldom ever went. This habit caught up with them till almost no day passed by without another bill collector calling to demand money.

Phil and Bonnie suffered from these severe money problems in spite of the fact that they both enjoyed high-paying jobs. Deciding that they had to do something to solve their money problems, they made an appointment to see me.

Since they had been in the habit of playing the game of avoiding all financial realities, I spent the first session helping them face the stark reality of exactly where they were financially. There are so many people who will never be helped in their financial situation, not because they cannot learn how to help themselves, but because they continue to play the game of avoiding financial realities. The longer people play this game and the older they get the sadder it is.

To get Phil and Bonnie to take an honest look at where they were financially I had them do two financial exercises, which I want you to do also.

You will need two blank sheets of paper and a pencil or pen. Before proceeding to do exercise 1 take a good look at Phil and Bonnie's example given here:

Example of Exercise No. 1

ASSETS:

Savings in U.S. National	$ 480.
Checking Account	46.
Prepaid Insurance	254.
Value of Car	3,900.
Resale Value of Furniture	1,600.
Tax Evaluation of House	39,500.
TOTAL ASSETS	$45,780.

LIABILITIES:

Unpaid Balance on Car Loan	$ 3,600.
Home Loan	36,150.
Improvement Loan	2,000.
Finance Company	4,236.
Unpaid Medical Bills	810.
Note Due Grandfather	600.
Furniture Loan	700.
TOTAL LIABILITIES	$48,096.

TOTAL ASSETS	$45,780.
TOTAL LIABILITIES	−48,096.
TOTAL NET WORTH	$−2,316.

Take a piece of paper and make an evaluation of where you are financially today. For one heading write "Assets," and underneath list the amounts in your savings account, checking account, equity in a house, actual value of furniture, equity in car or cars, bonds, equity in any property owned, and any other assets you have. If you over-inflate your assets, you are kidding yourself.

For the second heading write the word "Liabilities." Here list all of your indebtedness—what you owe the bank, finance company, credit union, child support, unpaid balance on credit cards, medical bills, and any other indebtedness you have incurred.

To determine your net worth: subtract your total liabilities from your total assets and you will have your up-to-date net worth. If you have more assets than you have liabilities you are in the plus column. If you have more indebtedness than you have assets, your financial situation desperately needs your attention. When you are increasing your net worth every year you are moving ahead financially. When your net worth is decreasing, you are declining financially.

I said to Phil and Bonnie that the next step in taking an honest look at where they were financially was to do exercise No. 2 and discover what their monthly cash flow was.

Here is an example of a monthly cash flow exercise as this young couple completed it:

Example of Exercise No. 2

CREDITORS	TOTAL UNPAID BALANCE	MONTHLY PAYMENT
Car Loan	$ 3,600.	$112.
Home Loan	36,150.	366.
Improvement Loan	2,000.	37.
Finance Co.	4,236.	256.
Medical Bill	810.	37.
Furniture Loan	700.	43.
TOTAL MONTHLY PAYMENT		$861.

TOTAL MONTHLY INCOME		$1,427.
TOTAL MONTHLY PAYMENT		−861.
TOTAL MONTHLY CASH FLOW		$ 566.

As you can see from the example, although this young couple had a good income, after debt payment they had only $566 per month to live on.

Now let's proceed to discover what your monthly cash flow is after debt payments have been made.

On your second sheet of paper once again list by name each of your lenders. Having completed the list, leaving out no one to whom you owe money, write beside each lender the amount of your monthly payment.

Once you have completed your personal monthly debt payment list, take one deep breath and move ahead with courage to add up the amount you are obligated to pay each month. Inasmuch as you have come this far you may as well go ahead and face all the reality.

Write down the total of your monthly income. Then underneath it write once again the figure representing your total monthly debt payment. Subtract your total monthly debt payment from your total monthly income. The figure you have left represents your own monthly cash flow.

The harsh financial reality is that an awful lot of people have a minus cash flow. What this sad state of financial affairs means is that when all monthly debt payments are made there is no money left for even the bare essentials like food.

In good financial management one will never obligate himself for any debt without making doubly sure that his cash flow will be sufficient to not only care for the necessities of life but for the emergencies as well as extra goodies. The amount you have left after debt payments, your cash flow, is of far more consequence to everyday living than the amount of your income. No matter how much you make, if you have nothing left to call your own, what good is your income?

I am convinced that, as you apply the good financial principles from Scripture we are learning together in this book, you will greatly increase your monthly cash flow.

2. *Define your financial objectives and purposes.* One of the most profitable things we have ever done in our church was to spend several sessions together as a board of directors in order to hammer out in eight concise sentences what our objectives are as a church.[1] As pastor, I manage our church by these objectives! In addition, we have set our long-range goals, our intermediate goals, and our short-range goals, all in keeping with our main objectives. I hire staff members and plan programs that are in line with fulfilling our primary objectives as a church. These objectives keep us headed in the right direction, making the most of our efforts, and accomplishing the things that we most want to accomplish.

Before one can achieve the financial success he desires he must crystallize his objectives and set clearly defined goals. Objectives are broad purposes; goals are measurable, accomplishable, specific things. To be truly a successful person financially you will want to choose both objectives and goals which will help you to fulfill the plans and purposes of God for your life.

In keeping with God's plan for my life, here are my four financial objectives:

- to provide well for my family;
- to do whatever I can to advance the cause of Jesus Christ;
- to become financially independent in the years to come;

43

- to increase and multiply what God places in my care.

3. *Set long-range financial goals.* One powerful word in the English language has only three letters: A-I-M. We get exactly what we aim for. Humans have a marvelous capacity to move right on course toward what they are aiming for. Many people have little or nothing financially because that's what they have aimed for. The big difference between those who achieve great things and those who don't achieve anything is that those who achieve set big goals and put forth the extra effort over a long period of time to achieve their goals. That's the difference. It is not that one person is smarter than the other or has more talent or more ambition or more opportunity—it's just that he has taken the time to visualize his goals and has aimed his life toward the achievement of what he wants.

The first man to walk on the moon, Neil Armstrong, was raised in the town of Wapakoneta, Ohio. In Wapakoneta, Neil is remembered as a youth who fulfilled all the ideals of what you would expect of a typical American boy. Under his picture in the high school yearbook were these words: "He thinks, he acts, 'tis done." Way back there, years ago, they were prophesying a great future for him. He was especially good at science and mathematics.

One night in the spring of his senior year in high school, according to a newspaper account, he stopped by to visit with his physics and chemistry teacher, Mr. Krite. After an enjoyable evening together, it came time for Neil to leave. Teacher and student stepped out on the porch together. Above them the great silvery moon was bathing the earth in all its glory. As they stood there admiring the breathtaking moon together, Mr. Krite said, "Neil, you're a good boy. Tell me, what are you going to do with your life.?"

Neil smiled, looked up at the moon, and said, "Mr. Krite, some day I plan to visit that man up there."

The teacher smiled, thinking, "Poor Neil, he'll always be a dreamer."

That was back in 1946, when no one had any thought of going to the moon. But Neil Armstrong did it. He was the first man on the moon, but long before he achieved, he had a great goal. Remember, there is tremendous power in having great long-range goals.

Sit down and write out on paper your long-range financial goals. These should be the financial accomplishments that you choose to work toward during the next 20 years. There's nothing like a great goal to bring the best out of a person. As an example, here are my own long-range financial goals:

- to help build Oregon's first walk-in, drive-in church;
- to be in a position financially to assist my children in completing their higher education;
- to own a large family home adequate to entertain Christian friends;
- to provide security for my wife throughout her lifetime;
- to be financially independent by retirement age even though I do not plan on ever retiring;
- to have enough extra money to enjoy some of the finer things in life.

4. *Set intermediate goals.* Write down the goals you want to achieve in the next three to five years. These should fit into your long-range goals and also should be

45

goals that you can begin working on even now. As an example, these are my intermediate goals:

- secure beginning investment properties;
- purchase larger family home;
- be free from all indebtedness except indebtedness incurred for investment purposes on property;
- give $10,000 gift above and beyond my regular tithes and offerings to help build Oregon's first walk-in, drive-in church.

5. *Set short-range goals.* Nothing will add any more zest to your daily life than having some immediate financial goals that you are working on. You don't have to wait until tomorrow. In fact, if tomorrow is to be what you want it to be, you must begin today. Break your larger goals into smaller parts and begin now to manage your finances by objectives. Adopt short-range goals that you want to achieve for the next 10 to 12 months. Write your goals on paper and keep them constantly before you.

In all your goal-setting, pray about your goals in order to be sure they are the right ones. Right financial goals will help you to realize and enjoy the abundant life that Christ came to give you. My own short-range goals for the next 10 to 12 months are:

- to pay off the loan on our car;
- to save 10 percent of our income;
- to plan and provide for a wonderful family vacation this summer;
- to give $1,000 above tithes for our church building fund.

6. *Possibilitize until you can see your desired goal.* For example, suppose we decide that it would take one million dollars in cash to have the kind of financial base

necessary to build Oregon's first walk-in, drive-in church. How does a congregation that is independent and has been in existence just three short years come up with a million dollars? On the surface, we would have to say it is impossible. What would it take to make possible the raising of a million dollars? Let's break it down and see:

- If someone would give a million dollars, it would be possible.
- If 10 people would give $100,000 each, it would be possible.
- If 100 people would give $10,000 each, it would be possible.
- If 200 people would give $500 each for the next 10 years, it would be possible.

Now I believe it is possible, because I see how it can be done.

How do you climb a mountain? One step at a time.

How do you achieve mountainous financial goals? Just like you eat an elephant—one bite at a time. You keep breaking it down until you have the smallest part, until you have a goal that you can work on and achieve now. After you have accomplished step one, you go to step two, then step three, then step four, and on and on until you get on top of your financial mountain.

7. *Set a definite day on which you expect to reach a goal.* Set up report-in days. In other words, every couple of months, on a predetermined date, sit down and evaluate how you are doing, how far you have come, how far you have to go. For good financial management make yourself accountable.

8. *Get the most for your time.* In the time that you have to produce income, are you spending it in the most

47

profitable way? As a pastor of an enlarging, thriving congregation, I cannot afford to spend time doing such things as running errands, running the mimeograph machine, and many of the other time-consuming details that other persons can do. This is why the first person we hired on our staff was an efficient secretary. This frees me to use my time in the most profitable ways. Time is money; it must be spent wisely.

No one has any more time than you do. Ask yourself this penetrating question: *How am I using my time?* Are you using your time to achieve your objectives, or are you allowing yourself to get bogged down in time-consuming detours off the main course? You can either make your time count or you can waste it. It's up to you to manage your own time.

Get Paid for Your Time

It is absurd what low wages some people work for, while people of equal or less ability are making much higher wages. Being well suited for a job is an essential consideration in your employment, but, all things being equal in job opportunities, it's much better to make a good wage than to keep squeaking by on a not-so-good wage. Why settle for less if, through personal initiative, you can do better?

It has been estimated that in America today 65 percent of women work outside the home. I know from years of counseling that some women are definitely better off working. They have a need to work in order to be fulfilled. In many cases, though, this question needs to be considered: Is it worth a mother's time to work outside the home? At the institute for successful marriage, which we hold annually at New Hope Community

Church, in one of the small group sessions on family finance, this amazing financial picture was presented in a discussion of the pros and cons of the working wife:

Cost per Week for a Working Mother

Federal income tax—20% min.	$ 20.00
State income tax	3.00
Social Security tax	5.20
Tithe	10.00
Transportation	10.00
Lunch and coffee breaks	7.00
Restaurants and carry-outs	12.00
Extra clothes	10.00
Forfeited savings on purchases	8.00
Hairdresser	5.00
Other "I-owe-it-to-myself" expenses	5.00
Employee insurance	3.00
Baby-sitting for two children	25.00
TOTAL EXPENSES	$123.20
GROSS INCOME PER WEEK	−100.00
COST TO HUSBAND	$ 23.20

Of far more consequence than how much money you make is what you are doing with what you are now earning. This is a tough truth for most of us to accept, but if we are to succeed financially, we must accept it. In the past year I have had close fellowship with several persons who are making six to ten times the average income, but who are always in financial hot water. One professional man, who has an immense income, seldom has a day go by without being phoned by some bill collector attempting to collect a bill far past due. A researcher has noted that families that make twice the

49

national average have greater problems paying their bills than families that make the national average.

You ask, "How can this be?" No matter what a person earns, it still comes down to the point of money management.

> WHETHER YOUR INCOME IS LARGE OR SMALL,
> OR SOMEWHERE IN BETWEEN,
> STEP OUT FROM THE CROWD,
> STAND UP TO YOUR GOD-GIVEN RESPONSIBILITY,
> AND MOVE AHEAD
> BY BECOMING THE MANAGER OF WHAT GOD GIVES YOU.

Footnote

1. *New Hope Community Church objectives and purposes:*
   Reach Unchurched Thousands
   Healing Center
   Edifying Center
   Equipping Center
   Build Strong Christian Families
   Christ Center of Positive Inspiration
   Deploying Center
   Worship Center

4
HOW TO DO AWAY WITH DEPRESSING DEBTS

There is no depression to compare with debt depression; it is a heavy oppression all its own. It would be impossible to measure all the mental anguish, the sleepless nights, the unhappy homes, and the countless heartaches caused by depressing debts. Insurance companies tell us that people who are heavily in debt are especially accident-prone. Those who analyze workers' ability to produce on the job tell us that those suffering from depressing debts are not as productive in their work. You see, *debts are extremely costly!*

One man who was heavily in debt said, "I feel like a frightened, trapped animal caught in the jaws of a giant debt trap." I have yet to meet an individual who intended to get caught in the jaws of a giant debt trap. I have yet to meet an individual who intended to get caught in the squeeze of the debt trap, but sales pitches are so alluring and easy payment plans are made to look so easy that one can fall into the debt trap and be caught almost before he knows it. And once debt has a firm hold on you, it accelerates like an 18-wheel truck that has lost its brakes, going downhill faster and faster at a terrifying, out-of-control speed.

What is debt? It is money you have already spent that you never really had. But now, whether or not you have the money, you must pay back what you have borrowed, plus interest. The hard-hitting truth is that *now*, in order to pay what you have *already spent*, you must live not only on what you are making but on *less* in order to come up with the extra money you need for debt payment.

There is no getting around it—money that you borrow and spend today you are going to have to sacrifice doubly in order to repay it in the days ahead. All of us remember that, as kids, when we wanted something to happen (such as Christmas) it seemed like tomorrow would never come. Well, when it comes to paying back debts, tomorrow always comes too soon! Tomorrow becomes *today* before very many hours have passed. It is like the last words in a children's hide-and-seek game: "Ready or not, here I come!"

Debts on depreciating items like furniture, clothing, food, gasoline, appliances, or an automobile *are not God's will for you!* These kinds of losing debts violate God's directive "Keep out of debt altogether" (Rom. 13:8, *Phillips*). Our heavenly Father, earnestly desiring what is best for us, warns that indebtedness makes us slaves, even though He created us to be free. "Just as the rich rule the poor, so the borrower is servant to the lender" (Prov. 22:7, *TLB*). *Financial freedom is what God wants for you!*

When my wife and I got married we had a better-than-average income with both of us working. With the 12 charge accounts we had between us and the large car payment at a high rate of interest—it was a discouraging thing indeed to sit down once a month and attempt to keep up with all these payments, even though we had a very good income. By skimping and scraping we could barely make all these payments. At this rate Margi would be teaching school for the rest of her life instead of just to the end of the year. We decided right then and there that we'd better start out our newfound life together with managing our money.

One family I worked with had $4000 in short-term debts. Their payments of $225 a month had to be made out of a take-home pay of $750. This left them with $525 a month to support a family of five. Needless to say, they were having a tough time keeping afloat, and were doing so only by scrimping on some very basic necessities. A long time ago the extras had to go—no more vacations and no meals out. How do families like this get into such a fix? By falling into the easy credit trap.

Here is what Margi and I did about our financial pinch. We got out our 12 credit cards and had a little ceremony. We took the scissors and had lots of fun cutting the cards into little pieces. We made a vow to each other that we would never again charge anything, but would pay cash. The first six months, as I remember, were really tough. It was like climbing a hill but never reaching the top. It meant going without some things that we had been used to buying on charge accounts. However, together we stuck to it.

I remember that about the sixth month we paid off two of the charge accounts completely. Then we found that we had more money to work with the next month, so we could pay more on the remaining accounts. It was an exciting snowball effect. Every time we paid off an account, the next month we had more money to pay on other debts. We also sold our big, expensive car and bought a more moderately priced one, which was more in keeping with our objectives and goals.

Within one year we had all the short-term debts paid off. As a result, Margi was able to stop teaching school to devote her full time to sharing in my ministry. We were now in a financial position that allowed me to resign my steady income and launch out into the beginning of the ministry of New Hope Community Church. All of this was possible because we became the managers of the money that God had given us.

You too can get on top of your debts. Be wise like an owl, and stay away from the credit trap. Decide to buy very few items on time (a house, maybe a car), and never run large charge accounts at stores or borrow at high rates of interest.

Who can afford to pay 18 percent interest? *If you can't afford to pay cash now, how can you afford to pay cash plus the 18 percent interest tomorrow?* You don't have to drown in debt. You can do something better; with determination and discipline, you can get on top.

If you are one of the many that are drowning in depressing debt, my heart goes out to you. For you, God has a better way to live. Jesus said, "I am come that they might have life, and that they might have it more abundantly" (John 10:10, *KJV*). Too many Christians are being robbed of inner peace and happiness simply because they have followed the ways of men by falling headlong into the debt trap. For you, God has something better than to go on drowning yourself in debt depression. The time has come for you, with Christ's help, to change your financial situation. I believe you can do it because of this power-packed Bible promise: "I can do all things through Christ which strengtheneth me" (Phil. 4:13, *KJV*).

Ten Ways to Get Out of Depressing Debt

1. Face the facts of how much your heavy debt is costing you. Anytime a person refuses to face the facts of his situation, things always continue to get worse, never better. Before things can get better for you, you need to face the facts. As you face your situation, ask these questions: How many dollars must I pay each month in debt payments alone? Am I paying all my bills each month, or am I going in the hole continually? After all my bills are paid each month, how much cash do I have left over? What emotional effects are my debts having on me and my family?

Recently while I was counseling with a young couple about their depressing financial situation, they asked me this question: "How did we ever get ourselves into such a debt mess?" I said, "It is easy. Multitudes of people are doing it all the time." This is how they do it:

a. Follow the crowd.
b. Use credit cards and don't pay the entire balance each month. Just allow the unpaid balance to go higher and higher at 18 percent interest a year.
c. Spend more money than you make.
d. Abuse and misuse credit.
e. Make the mistake of borrowing money for things that soon have little or no cash value left.

If you are drowning in depressing debt, the very best

thing you can do is this: Right now, pray and turn all your finances over to Someone who is bigger than you are—God. Read the Bible, paying special attention to the book of Proverbs, and then do exactly what God tells you to do. (Prov. 3:6,9,10,27,28; 5:11; 6:1,6–11; 10:16,26; 11:15; 14:8; 15:22,27; 16:8,11; 17:18; 20:16; 21:20; 22:3,4,7,9,22,23; 23:4,5; 24:3,4,27; 27:13; 28:13, 22,25.)

2. *Make up your mind that with God's help you are going to become a debt-free person.* Until an individual decides that he wants to become free from depressing debt, he will go right on down the same old muddy river of debt. He will always feel like the victim when he could be the victor. If your debt situation is to be changed in the future, you must decide to do something now. *I believe that with God's help you can overcome depressing debt.* Make this Achiever's Creed your prayer:

WHATEVER THE MIND CAN CONCEIVE,
AND I WILL DARE TO BELIEVE,
WITH GOD'S HELP I CAN ACHIEVE![1]

3. *Declare a moratorium on adding any additional debts.* Getting out of debt is not easy. If it were, everyone would do it. No one ever gets out of debt by simply wishing it would happen. To get out of debt means that you have to put a stop to spending more than you make. If you are really serious about getting out of debt, not only are you going to have to spend less, but you must declare a moratorium on all spending other than the bare necessities of life. The quicker you have the courage to do this, the sooner you get on your road to financial freedom. Let me warn you that getting out of debt is an uphill climb all the way. There is no easy way to

do it. *Getting out of debt means denying the lesser in order to gain the greater.*

Yes, working at getting out of debt takes extra effort. It is tough going, but the benefits from such self-denial and discipline is overwhelmingly worth it. You may not be able to accept it, but the truth is this: If this very day someone were to pay all your debts without you learning the lessons from struggling to repay your own debts, you would more than likely get into debt all over again. I am so happy for you, because even though the road to getting out of debt is going to be hard, you will learn one of the most valuable lessons of life, that of managing your money. Here are some of the other rewards that are yours to gain:

Peace of mind
Improved relationships with creditors
Better physical and emotional health
More harmonious family life
Self-respect
Freedom—glorious freedom

4. *Cut up all credit cards and throw them away.* After I had made this statement in a sermon one Sunday, a lady came up and said, "Don't you think that is a little radical to do?"

I said, "Yes, it is! But if you have a radical debt problem, and if you are to find a solution, it requires some very radical action." So, as I see it, if it is your credit cards that have helped get you into financial difficulty, then it makes good sense to get rid of that which has contributed to your delinquency.

Let me explain that I am not against credit cards. My father, for example, as a church administrator had to travel many miles. It was more preferable for him to use

57

credit cards than to carry cash. However, to my father's praise, he was a very disciplined man who managed his money and paid his charges within the 30 days due without having to suffer interest penalties. Eighteen percent, the standard credit card interest rate, is pretty heavy interest in anybody's book. *If you cannot afford to pay cash now, can you afford to pay later with interest?*

Legitimately someone will point to his need of having credit cards in order to establish identity or to cash a check. It's true that a lot of places not only require a driver's license but an additional credit card or two.

Consequently, my wife and I, after having taken the debt cure by disposing of all credit cards, have now learned to manage our money to the degree that we can trust ourselves to carry one or two credit cards for the very purpose of identification. The point is, don't tempt yourself beyond your own ability to manage. Don't kid yourself into thinking you won't use credit cards when you always do. In our case, in order to resist the old temptation to overspend by charging on credit cards, we carry credit cards that are usable in one store only, such as Sears or Penney's. Away from these stores, the cards are useful only for identification.

Quite frankly, my advice to you is this: If you are experiencing depressing debt as a result of the misuse of credit cards, then admit you have not had the discipline to properly use them and take whatever radical action is called for to climb out of the hurting debt trap. "When a bird sees a trap being set, it stays away" (Prov. 1:17, *TLB*). If you have the debt problem, the sooner you take the credit card cutting remedy, the quicker you are going to solve your debt problem.

5. *Have a sale.* Ask yourself what you have of value that is not a necessity, what things you can sell and convert into cash. Then take the cash and use it to reduce your indebtedness and in some cases even wipe out all debts. There are a lot of things we want that, if we are really honest, we can do without.

The Hedges were more than $4000 in debt when they came to see me, and were far behind in many of their monthly debt payments. As we talked, John, who was a very sincere Christian, grasped the insight that this kind of indebtedness was not God's will for him. At that point he gave up clinging to the truck that he liked so well but could not afford, and he committed himself to selling it. Within a couple of days the truck was sold, and this family's total indebtedness was reduced in half. Their monthly cash flow actually increased to the point that they had $100 left each month after everything was paid.

Phil and Judy DuFresne had been Christians for only two years when they made up their minds to seek out God's best in the area of their financial life.

Phil worked long and hard hours as a truck driver, but, in spite of making fabulous money, Phil told me he felt like he was working all the time for the credit union, and he found this to be very depressing. Twice a month, when his bills were paid out of his paycheck, there was little or nothing left. Phil found himself very frustrated over working so hard and not having any money, and by his own admission he too often took his frustration out on his wife and kids. Let's face it—to work hard and not have anything left the day after payday makes one up-tight!

I asked Phil, "Why do you think you allowed yourself

59

to become overextended financially?" This is what he said: "It was the lack of the Lord in my life. I don't know quite how to say this, but I loved for people to look at me and say, 'Man, look at what he's got. He's really something. Wow! I wish I had what he's got.' I really enjoyed people's attention. It was an awful merry-go-round, because all the material things we bought never gave us any lasting satisfaction."

Phil and Judy had received much financial instruction from the Bible as they attended our church. They had heard other people joyfully testify to becoming debt-free, but they didn't decide to do anything about their own problem until one day they looked at their credit union coupon book and faced the fact that they owed $4900. At that moment they faced the reality of the huge sum of money that was taken out of every pay-check just to meet the monthly credit union payment. Phil said, "I just could not believe it." Out loud he said, "Man, this is unreal! Here I am making good money, but with payments like this I don't have any money left. Something has got to be done to change this."

Their decision to do something was further cemented when they calculated that they had paid $795 in interest during the last year on this huge debt!

Phil told me, "You know, I had a truck, a camper, and a boat, and I liked them all a whole lot. I liked to do things in style, but the Lord showed me that if I would sell these three things, I could be debt-free except for my house payment."

Being a man of action, Phil had a sale and gave up the three things that meant a lot to him in order to achieve something greater that he wanted much more. With the cash from the sale, Phil and Judy not only wiped out the

$4900 owed to the credit union, but they paid off their credit cards to boot. Their glowing testimony was that because they paid off their debts, they now enjoy 400 additional dollars per month in their cash flow!

During an interview in one of our financial management seminars, Phil gave this advice for people who were caught in the debt trap but wanted to get free. "Well, I think first of all you have to make the decision that you want to do something to change it. I think that when a person is heavily in debt, as we were, you are enslaved to material things. The devil has you right where he wants you. It's really a defeating thing to be so heavily in debt. He likes to see you get overextended so that he can get your family into a mess. I believe that Jesus wants you to be free. If you will obey Him, He will help you become free."

Then, with tears streaming down his face, Phil bragged on Judy and their children for their cooperation and help in this major financial achievement.

Phil put the icing on the cake of our interview when he described what the overcoming of debt had done for his marriage: "There is a closeness now that we didn't have before. When I come home, I'm not all tense like I was. I feel like I have accomplished something. I have worked that day for something—not for the credit union, but for my family."

6. *Set a monthly debt reduction goal.* You should make this amount as large as you possibly can, yet you should be realistic about your everyday needs.

I will never forget one couple who came to see me for financial help. Although young, they had actually given up hope of ever getting out of debt, because they were being buried beneath a $6000 avalanche of debt. In despondency and desperation they laid out all their debts on the table. Right then I helped them devise a plan of attack. Together we set a realistic monthly debt reduction goal. I showed them that, if they followed this consistently and persistently, they would actually have all their debts paid off within 18 months. The beauty of hope broke out in a smile on their faces. They even showed excitement, because now they had a plan that they could follow in order to become debt-free.

Though they left my office with high expectations, they didn't reach their goal in 18 months. I don't know whether I miscalculated or they made a few mistakes along the way and didn't follow the plan as closely as they might have. But what a celebration it was when in 24 months they came to see me and announced with great pride that they were now debt-free. Believe it— you too can become debt-free!

7. *Use all extra income to pay off your depressing debts.* One thing is for sure—you don't want to keep those depressing debts hanging around your neck. Hasten your day of financial freedom by making the commitment in advance to add all extra income to debt repayment.

Wise is the man who heeds this admonishment from the Scriptures: "Don't withhold repayment of your debts. Don't say 'some other time,' if you can pay now" (Prov. 3:27,28, *TLB*).

Last month Margi and I received $1000 from a sale. Immediately we had the old impulse to go out and buy something. To spend the money on the new drapes that we had been desiring certainly looked like an inviting expenditure. But because of the truth of Scripture and our commitment to follow it, I took the $1000 into our bank and paid it on our car loan. The Bible tells us to pay our debts first, not because we want to but because it is the right thing to do. And you know, we experienced a lasting feeling of joy from knowing that we had almost eliminated our last depreciating debt.

The next time you receive an income tax return, a raise in pay, a bonus, cash from a sale, or any other extra income, what are you going to do with it? If you allow your emotional urges to rule you, you'll probably buy something you don't really need. But if you are committed to getting out of debt and making good use of the mind God has given you, you will seize the opportunity to reduce your indebtedness.

8. *Get started today.* Wishful thinking will never get you out from under depressing debt. Begin to work your plan, not *tomorrow* but *now*. Someone has said, "Beginning is half done." So the sooner you get going, the sooner you will be free and clear.

9. *Make whatever financial sacrifices are necessary to achieve your goal of being debt-free.* There is no way of getting around it—realizing goals means discipline. It is true that the best things in life cost the most. There has never been an athlete, an executive, an inventor, a pastor, or anyone else who has succeeded without paying a price. Your price to be free from imprisoning debt is to use personal discipline, to give up the lesser things to achieve the greater goal. This means being selective, saying no to impulse buying. It means self-denial, sticking by your guns. Your goal of being free from depressing debt is a worthy one, so keep it always before you.

The more worthwhile the goal, the greater the obstacle. I know there are going to be all kinds of obstacles along the way in your goal of becoming free from debt, but God will be with you if you ask Him. "I can do all things through Christ, which strengtheneth me." The best things take effort, time, and Jesus' help.

10. Be determined. More than likely you did not get heavily into debt overnight. It took weeks, months or years. By the same token, neither can you expect to get out of debt suddenly. No doubt it will take days, weeks, months, or even years for you to become debt-free. But be willing to take however long it takes. *Practice Patience.*

Whatever you do, *don't give up.* One of the most common causes of failure is the habit of quitting when one is overtaken by temporary setbacks. It is not going to be easy for you to get out of debt, but stick with it and never give up. Those who never give up become free persons. With Christ's help you are going to be free from depressing debt.

With Jesus Christ you can overcome anything and everything, including depressing debts. Make this your prayer:

I CAN GET OUT OF DEBT
THROUGH CHRIST, WHO STRENGTHENS ME.

Footnote

1. Dale E. Galloway, *Dream a New Dream*, (Wheaton, Illinois: Tyndale House, 1975) p. 57.

5

WHEN TO BORROW AND WHEN NOT TO BORROW

In Dr. Robert Schuller's book *Your Church Has Real Possibilities*, he tells his famous "never borrow money for coal" story. I have heard him tell it at the Institute for Successful Church Leadership, which he holds several times a year in Garden Grove, California. Here is Dr. Schuller's story, which will help you see when to borrow and when not to borrow:[1]

Never Borrow Money for Coal

When I left Western Seminary and went to my first pastorate in Chicago, Illinois, I lived in the church parsonage. It was heated with coal, and when October came, I needed coal for the furnace. One of the men in the church said, "Well, it'll take about five tons of coal to get you through the winter. At fifteen dollars a ton, that's seventy-five dollars."

I didn't have seventy-five dollars, so I called up the coal yard and asked, "Will you deliver five tons of coal?"

"Yes."

"Will you charge it, please?"

"Oh, we don't charge coal."

"You're kidding."

"Oh, no, not at all. Guess you'll have to borrow it from the bank."

I hung up.

At the bank, I asked, "Would you loan me money for coal?"

"Oh, no," the banker replied, "We don't loan money for coal." What he didn't say, and what he meant was, "You're only twenty-two years old and you're new at all this, so you don't know any better." Then the banker said, "I tell you what, Rev. Schuller. I'll loan you money for coal this time, but never again."

"Why not?" I asked.

"Well," he explained, "you will burn up that coal. If you don't pay us back our seventy-five dollars, what do we get in return? Nothing—it's all gone up in smoke."

That banker then gave me some of the soundest advice I've ever received: "Never borrow money for coal. You want to borrow money for a car—for a house—come to us. And all we will say is, 'Can you make the monthly payments?' If you've got the cash, or the salary coming in to make the monthly payments, we'll loan you money on that house or car.

"Then if you can't pay the mortgage back, we take the house or the car and sell it. If there's any money left over after we get paid, you get it. We call that equity.

"But," he went on, "never borrow money for the gasoline you put in the car. Never borrow money for the tires you put on the car. Never borrow money for the spark plugs. *Never borrow money for coal.*"

Now that's a fundamental principle. We borrow money for this church, but we don't borrow money for coal! We borrow money for everything that has collateral, non-depreciable value. But we don't borrow money for our television ministry, for interest on the capital debt, for salaries or for utilities. That's coal money. That's gasoline. That's tires.

Additional Tips on Borrowing Money

1. Don't borrow money until you have sufficient cash flow to make the payments.

2. Borrow money only when you *can* afford to borrow and *can't* afford not to borrow.

3. Borrow money when it is going to make you money.

4. Borrow money when it is going to increase your net worth over a period of time.

5. Borrow money when it saves you money.

6. Borrow money when it is going to increase your earning power. For example, borrowing money for your

education may be a very sound thing for you to do.

Before You Borrow, Go on a Money Shopping Spree

As the late Dale Carnegie used to say, "Where your money is concerned you are in business for yourself." It pays to shop around for the lowest rate of interest before you borrow. Loan fees and interest rates charged by different lending institutions vary widely.

Six years ago, when I purchased a car, I made the mistake of allowing the sales manager to talk me into taking a loan through their line of credit. Only later did I have the rude awakening that I had signed for a loan that was costing me 14 percent interest! A couple of years after that, a little older and much wiser, when purchasing a car I shopped around to get the lowest rate of interest. I found a local bank in which, by putting one-third down, I was able to obtain a loan at only 7½ percent interest!

When it comes to borrowing money, bargain wherever you can, for after all it is for your best interest. The loaning of money is a very competitive business. Home mortgages may vary as much as 2 percent in your area. Over the life of the average home loan (25 to 30 years), this difference adds up to thousands of dollars. By being a wise borrower you can save yourself plenty of money.

Be aware that the same bank or lending institution may charge different rates, depending on the person and circumstances. Always try to keep yourself in a position where you can demand, in a kind but firm way, the very best rate you can.

Stay away from finance companies that charge up to 36 percent for loans under $300 and 18 percent for loans over $2500. If you don't qualify for a loan from those lenders who give the best rates, then, if at all possible, go without this extra money until you can make a better deal.

Finally, never borrow from anyone who charges an excessive interest rate; and never borrow unless you can get a complete copy of the contract note you must sign. Always require and receive a truth-in-lending form before you sign your name. Before signing your name on any contract, make sure that there are no spaces that have been left blank.

When borrowing money, be smart, shop around, and find the best bargain you can. Remember that every dollar you save on interest is another dollar you get to keep for yourself.

> DON'T BE AFRAID OF DEBT,
> BUT UNDERSTAND WHAT DEBT IS.[2]

Footnotes

1. Robert H. Schuller, *Your Church Has Real Possibilities* (Glendale, Calif.: G/L Publications, Regal Books Division, 1974), pp. 27,28.
2. Schuller, *Your Church Has Real Possibilities*, p. 27.

⑥
THE BITTER MIRACLE CURE FOR MONEY ILLS

It is a greater miracle drug than penicillin! It is something that everybody who handles money desperately needs to take, but which no one wants to swallow. What is this miracle drug, this bitter pill that has proven repeatedly to be the miracle-cure medicine for common money ills? *It is called a budget!*

Have you ever had the problem of money going through your hands like flour through a sifter? I have. Have you ever come to the end of the day and wondered what happened to all the cash you had in your billfold at the beginning of the day? I have. It is so easy to spend a few dollars here and there until, before you know it, you have blown a whole bunch of money and are surprised at the end of the day that you have nothing to show for it.

71

Most of the half-million dollars you will earn in your lifetime you will spend. You will either spend it wisely as a result of good planning or you will spend it carelessly, without thought or preplanning. In order to get the most out of your money, to make it go as far as possible, to get what you really want, you must have a built-in guidance system to guide you to your goal. To me this is exactly what a budget is: a programmed guidance system to keep us on target and assure us of reaching our financial goals.

Taking the time to plan what you will do with your money has far more to do with good financial results than the amount of money you earn. This is why the Scriptures tell us to plan: "Any enterprise is built by wise planning, becomes strong through common sense, and profits wonderfully by keeping abreast of the facts" (Prov. 24:3,4, *TLB*).

When people fall into financial difficulty, they usually think they are there because of the accidents, the wrecked car, the leaking roof, the medical bills, and on and on. But the truth is that the majority of people do not get into financial trouble by accident; they get there by default, by failing to plan ahead for inevitable unseen expenses. "A prudent man foresees the difficulties ahead and prepares for them; the simpleton goes blindly on and suffers the consequences" (Prov. 22:3, *TLB*).

Set Up a Budget to Plan Ahead—Now!

A workable budget is the only means I know for an individual or family to control their spending. If you had a leak in your roof and water was pouring all over your living room furniture, I know you would do something immediately to stop the leak! Almost all money woes are caused by uncontrolled spending. The way to stop the money leaks is to get a budget and use it to stop uncontrolled spending.

In setting up a personal budget there are a variety of acceptable forms from which to choose. The important point to remember is this: Select that form of budget that best suits your income and expenditures and is workable for you. In order to illustrate the usefulness of a budget, here is a sample form.

MONTH OF _____

FIXED EXPENSE	AMOUNT ALLOCATED	AMOUNT SPENT	DIFFERENCE (+ OR −)	UP-TO-DATE STATEMENT
House				
Auto Payment				
Contributions				
Savings				
Debts (long)				
Insurance				
Medical				

VARIABLE EXPENSES				
Utilities				
Phone				
Clothes				
Household				
Transportation				
Personal				
Recreation				
Miscellaneous				
Food				
TOTALS	$	$	$	$

Here is how to use the budget form:

1. The budget has been divided into two sections:

73

FIXED and VARIABLE expenses. Fixed expenses seldom, if ever, change in a year's time.

2. In the AMOUNT ALLOCATED column, list every expense under the appropriate heading. Under *Miscellaneous*, include newspapers, postage, etc. *Household* includes every expenditure for the house, both interior and exterior: tools, furniture, appliances, etc.

3. Allocate X number of dollars for each area of need. Your total allocation *must not exceed your net income.* (Net means money after all deductions.)

4. At the end of the month, total all your expenses and tabulate in AMOUNT SPENT column. This column is your control device. Some areas may be difficult to control. Be flexible, but never let total expenditure exceed income.

5. In the *difference column, record the exact amount over and under* AMOUNT ALLOCATED.

6. UP-TO-DATE STATEMENT is a running total of combined months. Looking at this column tells the budgeter where he stands over the year. For example, you might allocate $50.00 for clothing. The first month you spend $30.00, leaving a surplus of $20.00. If this occurs for six consecutive months, the UP-TO-DATE STATEMENT column would reveal that $120.00 extra was available.

Every successful budget has at least this one feature: *The income is greater than the expenditures.* Where there is no budget, more often than not the person keeps spending more money than he is making, and the results are like an automobile going down the highway out of control—a terrible accident is in the making. Become a responsible financial driver by making and *managing* your own personal budget. *Manage* your budget and you will avoid many a painful financial accident.

Give Family Members a Budget to Live Within

In our family I happen to get paid each Sunday, so every Monday when I go to the bank there's a certain amount of cash that I always get, while the rest is put into the checking and savings accounts. This cash is a predetermined amount that my wife and I have agreed on, which is in keeping with what I make and with our needs.

I have a budgeted amount that I use to pay for my own gasoline, car expenses, clothing, business lunches and recreation. Each week my wife, Margi, receives her share of the cash. What she does with it is up to her. I have asked her to take the responsibility of purchasing food and clothing for herself and the children and of managing the household expenses. If through thrift and good planning there is any excess, it is hers to do with as she sees fit.

I am a firm believer that a wife should not have to beg for her money, but should be given a fair portion of the family income that she is responsible to manage. On the other hand, it should be made clear that she is expected to live within her agreed-upon allotted income. By the same token, the husband should live within a fixed budget. When there are exceptions, this should be talked over openly and in a spirit of love and cooperation.

Be Firm and Stick by Your Guns

We have some close friends who have three teenagers in their home. It is a home that we enjoy being in a great deal because of their beautiful Christian hospitality. On one occasion when we were there recently, I overheard one of the children asking when they were going to get their clothing allowance. I asked the parents what this had reference to, and I was delighted to learn that they had placed each one of their teenagers on an assigned budget.

At the beginning of every month, each of the teens is given a set amount of money, out of which they are expected to buy their school lunches, their own clothing, and whatever other things they need. Each teen has been told that it is his responsibility to budget his own money. And when they are broke, they're broke. However, if through thrift and good money management they accumulate an excess, it is all theirs.

This wise father told me that before they started this plan it seemed like he was doling out money all the time for this and that and something else. But now he is actually spending less, and as an extra bonus his teenagers are learning how to manage their own money.

As you work your budget, expect some pain along the way. The path to financial success is not easy, nor is financial success to be gained without a great deal of effort.

Making a budget and sticking with it is probably the most difficult step to take in responsible financial management. Living under the control of a budget takes discipline and the courage to say no when you feel like saying yes.

In everyday living, keep in mind that your budget is not designed to *hurt* you but to *help* you; not to *enslave* you but to *free* you; not to *deprive* you but to *give you the best*. When you gain financial freedom instead of financial failure, you will thank God for your budget.

YOUR BUDGET IS YOUR TOOL TO HELP YOU
DENY THE LESSER IN ORDER TO GAIN THE GREATER.

7
SECRETS FOR YOUR FINANCIAL SUCCESS

You need money! I need money! Everybody needs money!

For every problem there is a solution, and *there is a solution to your money problems.* You are not the only one who knows your needs; God knows your needs and He knows my needs. Rest assured that God is not a disinterested being who has gone off and left us without solutions to our problems. In His love and presence He has given us financial principles in the Bible that can help us to be financially successful. It is the application of these biblical financial principles that can turn your life around and change it from lean to plenty, from want to abundance, from overwhelming problems to overflowing abundance.

How appropriate are the words of the First Psalm that

77

I memorized at my mother's knee, now made more clear in the up-to-date language of *The Living Bible:*

> "Oh, the joys of those who do not follow evil men's advice, who do not hang around with sinners, scoffing at the things of God: But they delight in doing everything God wants them to, and day and night are always meditating on his laws and thinking about ways to follow him more closely.
>
> "They are like trees along a river bank bearing luscious fruit each season without fail. Their leaves shall never wither, and all they do shall prosper."

Avoid These Causes of Financial Disaster

1. Avoid the pitfall of laziness. The Bible warns us against yielding to the temptation of giving in to laziness, because it leads to a life of poverty. Says the Bible, "A lazy man sleeps soundly—and goes hungry!" (Prov. 19: 15, *TLB*). "If you won't plow in the cold, you won't eat at the harvest" (Prov. 20:4, *TLB*). Additional verses in Proverbs that warn us against the foolishness of giving in to laziness are: Proverbs 12:27; 13:4; 15:19; 16:27; 19:24; 20:13; 21:25,26 (*TLB*).

It is easy to pick out the panhandlers in our society and say, "Hey, look at that lazy person!" It appears that whenever there is laziness, it is sooner or later followed by poverty and financial bondage. When there is no desire for gainful employment, one of the most loving things we can do to help motivate the person and help him become responsible is this: "If any would not work, neither should he eat" (2 Thess. 3:10, *KJV*).

Being honest with myself (which is not always easy to

do!), I have to admit that laziness is not just some foreign problem that the other guy has. It is something I must deal with and conquer within my own life. My problem is that on some mornings I don't even feel like getting out of bed. I have to kick myself out of the bed, get myself up, put myself in forward gear, and make myself go to work. As a minister I don't have a clock to punch. No one calls me and says, "Now go to work." If I would give in to my lesser desires, I would become lazy frighteningly quick. Before you can deal with something and overcome it, you have to admit that it is there. So let's admit it—there is a little bit of laziness in each of us.

Whenever people give in to laziness, they stay home when they could be going to work and making additional needed dollars for the family income. When a person gives in to laziness he does not put forth the extra needed effort to properly manage the dollars he has already worked hard to make. Give in to laziness and it will rob you of the financial success that God wants you to have. *So stand up to laziness and give it no opportunity to take over in your forward march toward financial success.*

2. Stay away from drunkenness and loose living. See drunkenness for what it is. It breaks my heart to see the poverty and feel the human suffering caused by alcoholism. Countless times I have seen firsthand the severe poverty and family suffering caused by drunkenness. How true are the words of the Bible, "A man who loves pleasure becomes poor; wine and luxury are not the way to riches!" (Prov. 21:17, *TLB*). *Drunkenness brings poverty.* "Don't carouse with drunkards and gluttons, for they are on their way to poverty" (Prov. 23:20,21, *TLB*). (See also Proverbs 23:29,30, *TLB*.)

Drunkenness and immorality not only cost people morally and spiritually, but they often result in financial ruin. Loose living seems to go together with loose spending. "For a prostitute will bring a man to poverty, and an adulteress may cost him his very life" (Prov. 6:26, *TLB*).

3. *Never allow your spending to exceed your income.* The plain truth is that you cannot spend more than you make and still be solvent financially. Ignore this truth and it will come back to haunt you sooner than you think. No matter how good the sale is or how super the buy appears to be, if buying it is going to make you spend more than you make, *you cannot afford the purchase.*

Here is a reality that you will be wise to accept: *No matter how much money a person makes, there is a limit to what he can spend.* Face the truth about your income; know what your limits are and decide to always stay within those boundary lines. So many people play the self-deception game, telling themselves they can afford something when they know good and well they cannot. Have the opennesss to admit when you cannot afford something, and have the good sense and courage to say, "I cannot afford it!"

For the best in money management always follow this rule: *Under no circumstances spend more money than you make.*

4. *Avoid playing the comparison game.* It never pays to look at what others have and to start desiring it. The Bible calls this coveting, but we in modern times call it "keeping up with the Joneses." Look at what the Joneses have—a new car, a new boat. We've got to have that too! Whenever people step into this pitfall they

almost always start buying for show, buying things they cannot afford but still not finding the peace and contentment that they secretly long for.

God created you uniquely different from anyone else. He never meant for you to compare yourself in any way to another person. Your worth as a person does not depend on what you own in comparison with your neighbors, but on the sole fact that God loves you as a member of His royal family. True contentment comes not from what you can get and possess, but from knowing that God possesses you and that you are His child. *As a child of God refuse to play the comparison game.*

5. *Avoid the debt trap like the plague.* This pitfall and how to avoid it, as well as how to overcome it, has been discussed in chapters 4 and 5.

6. *Avoid impulse buying.* If you are in financial straits, chances are that your buying habits put you there. Not only do we "do all kinds of wrong things to get money" (1 Tim. 6:9, *TLB*), but we also do all kinds of wrong things *with* money. Too often we buy with our emotions instead of with our intellect.

Last Christmas I had a strong emotional impulse to buy a Polaroid camera. I happened to have some extra money, so I went ahead and blew it all on this camera. I used the camera for a couple of days, but I hate to confess that I have not touched it since! Had I used my good sense before buying the camera, I would have admitted to myself that I really am not a camera bug and that after a few days I probably wouldn't take any further interest in photography.

By a little self-examination and honest answering, I would not have wasted my money buying something I wouldn't use after a few days.

The next time you are about to buy something, ask yourself these questions:

Do I need it?

Can I afford it?

Do I need something else more?

Can I get along well without it?

7. *Keep away from get-rich-quick schemes.* If someone is offering you something for nothing, you had better beware! The Bible states it this way: "Trying to get rich quick is evil and leads to poverty" (Prov. 28:22, *TLB*). "The man who wants to do right will get a rich reward. But the man who wants to get rich quick will quickly fail" (Prov. 28:20, *TLB*). There are no shortcuts to true and lasting rewards. *Gambling sooner or later always leads to financial ruin.* "Wealth from gambling quickly disappears; wealth from hard work grows" (Prov. 13:11, *TLB*).

8. *Be very careful about speculation.* Heed this verse: "Steady plodding brings prosperity; hasty speculation brings poverty" (Prov. 21:5, *TLB*). Thousands of years ago this was recorded in the book of Ecclesiastes about speculation: "The man who speculates is soon back to where he began—with nothing. This, as I said, is a very serious problem, for all his hard work has been for nothing; he has been working for the wind. It is all swept away. All the rest of his life he is under a cloud—gloomy, discouraged, frustrated, and angry" (Eccles. 5:15-17, *TLB*).

Unless you can afford to lose it, don't speculate, no matter how bright the prospects.

9. *Avoid the car payment until you are absolutely sure you can afford it.* The automobile is one item that keeps many families in financial hot water. How easy it is to

become disenchanted and discontent with your present car, and to go out and purchase a newer model that you cannot afford! Consumer reports tell us that few cars that are traded in are really worn out. Costs of repairs are usually minor compared to high monthly loan payments, and it is usually far more economical to keep your car in shape and run it into the ground, so to speak. Make sure you get the most out of the car you have.

So many financially troubled people that I counsel with have an extra car or truck that they cannot really afford to have. The truth is that a family has to have better-than-average income to afford that second car. If you feel financially squeezed and own more than one car in your family, the question you must ask yourself is this: Can we really afford that second car or that extra vehicle?

10. Be very slow to co-sign another person's note or to make a personal loan. At least six different times the book of Proverbs warns us not to loan money to unreliable people (for example, see Prov. 20:16, *TLB*). Whomever you loan money to, whether a friend at the time or not, one thing is sure—if he doesn't pay you back, he won't be your friend in the days to come! There is subtle temptation to allow debts to friends to slip by unpaid.

Concerning countersigning, "It is poor judgment to countersign another's note, to become responsible for his debts" (Prov. 17:18, *TLB*). "Unless you have the extra cash on hand, don't countersign a note. Why risk everything you own? They'll even take your bed!" (Prov. 22:26,27, *TLB*). "Be sure you know a person well before you vouch for his credit! Better refuse than suffer later" (Prov. 11:15, *TLB*).

11. Don't neglect to carry adequate insurance. The

right amount of insurance is this: What you can afford to live with if the emergency does not occur, and what you can afford to live with if the emergency happens.

12. Avoid being too proud to admit your own financial mistakes. Scores of people continue to get deeper and deeper into financial troubles simply because they are too proud to admit that they are making financial mistakes. But everyone makes financial mistakes, and wise is the man who admits these mistakes and learns from them. Foolish is the man who is too proud to admit what he is doing wrong financially. The Scripture warns, "Pride goes before destruction and haughtiness before a fall" (Prov. 16:18, *TLB*).

13. Overcome the temptation to think your money is going to manage itself. Fail to manage your money, and you plan to harvest financial failure.

The number one pitfall that multitudes of people have fallen into is the faulty thinking that somehow their money will manage itself. Nothing could be further from the truth. Don't be caught drifting along, hoping that by some magic your finances will suddenly all straighten out.

Did you ever think, "Boy, if someone would only leave me a large sum of money, then I'd not only pay all my indebtedness, but I would be on easy street"? Most of us who have ever been in a financial bind have dreamed of someone coming along and bailing us out. But did you know that most of the people who get bailed out by inheriting large sums of money blow it all in less than one year? That's right, at the end of the first year they have little or nothing to show for what they had inherited.

If you don't manage your money when you have little,

you won't manage it when you have more. To get the things you want out of life, you need to manage your money. To be successful financially, you must, with God's help, take a step out from the crowd and manage what you have, be it large or small. *I believe you can do it!*

Apply These Principles for Financial Success

1. Give 10 percent to God— off the top! The Bible calls this tithing. It happens to be a most important first step, not only in finding the solution to your money problems but also in becoming successful in the handling of all that God has given you, plus the increase He is going to bring to you as you put Him first.

To get God's best you have to give Him your best. Don't kid yourself—you can't give God leftovers and fool Him into thinking you are giving Him your best. There is no bigger fool than he who keeps fooling himself. You do want God's very best and highest in life, don't you? Then follow the teaching of Scripture found in Proverbs 3:6,9–11, *TLB:* "In everything you do, put God first, and he will direct you and crown your efforts with success. . . . Honor the Lord by giving him the first part of all your income, and he will fill your barns with wheat and barley and overflow your wine vats with the finest wines."

It has been my observation from working with hundreds of people that those who never learn to practice the principle of tithing are forever having multiple money problems. On the other hand, tithing alone does not guarantee financial success, but it is the most important beginning step to take in managing your money. And as you tithe you can count not only on God's help in your financial life but also on His bountiful blessings.

2. *Plan ahead by saving 10 percent regularly.* The Bible says, "A sensible man watches for problems ahead and prepares to meet them. The simpleton never looks, and suffers the consequences" (Prov. 27:12, *TLB*). (Also see Proverbs 22:3.)

In the passage of time you can reasonably expect some unforeseen financial emergencies. Sooner or later the roof is going to leak, or the tires on the car are going to get bald, or the car is going to need a major overhaul. So be wise, look ahead, and plan for the unseen inevitable. "The wise man looks ahead. The fool attempts to fool himself and won't face facts" (Prov. 14:8, *TLB*). *It pays to plan ahead.*

The only way to plan for future expenses is to start preparing by saving now. Recently a lady told me that when she became a Christian three years ago and received the challenge to become a tither, she accepted this challenge and started living off the remaining 90 percent. She said that after a while it seemed like she had as much money left as she had always had, so she thought to herself, "I'll take the next step. If I can give to God regularly and live off the 90 percent, then why can't I save 10 additional percent regularly and live off the 80 percent of income?" So she did this and now she was ecstatically telling me that, after several months of being on this regular saving program, she was getting along just marvelously. "The wise man saves for the future, but the foolish man spends whatever he gets" (Prov. 21:20, *TLB*).

3. *Adopt the "I can" attitude.* Someone has said, "Success comes in cans—*I can.*" On the other hand, say "I can't" and you have accepted failure as your lot with-

out even giving yourself a chance to succeed. Scores of people fail to lay hold of the treasures they could be enjoying simply because they settle for "I can't."

Henry Ford once said, "Think you can, think you can't. Either way you will be right." Others achieve success with their money; why can't you? Chances are that they aren't any smarter than you are—they simply believe they can become financial successes, and they work at it until what they believe happens. Believe me, becoming financially successful is worth your believing. You can!

4. Make up your mind to always be honest. Admittedly, evil men sometimes do prosper. Financial gain can sometimes be gotten through being dishonest. But this kind of gain is very temporary, like perishable produce. The Bible says, "A fortune can be made from cheating, but there is a curse that goes with it" (Prov. 20:21, *TLB*).

When you need to, remind yourself of this: There are no shortcuts to true financial success. Although you might obtain money by being dishonest, money received in this crooked way will not give you much lasting satisfaction.

5. Be diligent and work hard. Somebody has said, "There is no substitute for hard work. And there is no success for laziness." It is *working* that produces a crop of good things in a person's life.

How does your imagination feel today? Are you pretty good at using your imagination? I believe you are. Let's pretend you are age 16 again. (Don't you wish!) Do you remember how you wanted to impress that young man or that special girl? So what did you do? You spent hours combing your hair, polishing your shoes, dressing up, putting your best foot forward. Why does a member of one sex go to all that trouble to impress a member of the opposite sex? Because he wants to win her favor (or vice versa). He wants the best results.

To get the best in life you've got to put your best foot forward. Putting your best foot forward means working your hardest and putting your best efforts into whatever you are doing.

Do you want more of the good things in this world? Then work hard and you can have them. Listen to these words: "Work brings profit; talk brings poverty!" (Prov. 14:23, *TLB*). Other verses that promise good results from hard work are Proverbs 6:6-11; 12:24; 16:26; 22:29; and 28:19. One day I asked a successful Christian businessman how he achieved his success. He replied, "Being a Christian businessman is a full-time job. It requires hard work, sacrifice, and dedication. I believe Proverbs 12:11: 'Hard work means prosperity; only a fool idles away his time' " (*TLB*).

6. *Increase your ability to earn by taking advantage of opportunities to advance.* As a young man shared with me his exciting plans to further his education so he could advance into a better job, it gave me a burst of new enthusiasm for my day. The Bible says, "A wise youth makes hay while the sun shines, but what a shame to see a lad who sleeps away his hour of opportunity" (Prov. 10:5, *TLB*).

7. *Build your business first, before you build your house.* This wise truth is proclaimed in Proverbs 24:27. "Develop your business first, before building your house" (*TLB*). Other business advice is found in these verses: Proverbs 10:26; 14:4; 24:3,4; 26:13; and 27:23, 24. Make your business strong and productive first, and

then you will produce the needed income to build your house.

8. *Buy depreciable things only when you can pay cash.* This will be discussed in the next two chapters.

9. *Seek as much counsel and advice as you can get.* The person who seeks out expert financial advice before making a financial decision is going to be miles ahead. Some of the finest experts are more than willing to give counsel and help free of charge to those who seek it. The Bible says it this way: "A fool thinks he needs no advice, but a wise man listens to others" (Prov. 12:15, *TLB*). The more knowledgeable the people whose counsel you seek after and learn from, the wiser and more knowledgeable decision you will be able to make. As proven so many times, the person who thinks he knows it all is headed for trouble. "Plans go wrong with too few counselors; many counselors bring success" (Prov. 15: 22, *TLB*).

Not only is it good to seek out experts to give advice in their particular field, but is wise to seek counsel from mature, gifted Christians. For a spiritual man has understanding and good advice to give that the ungodly do not understand. "A godly man gives good advice ..." (Prov. 10:21, *TLB*). So often, others see what we do not see!

First and foremost before making a financial decision, seek God's guidance. The Bible tells us that His counsel is available for the asking. Listen to this terrific promise: "I will bless the Lord who counsels me; he gives me wisdom in the night. He tells me what to do" (Ps. 16:7, *TLB*).

10. *Before making a major financial decision, make sure you have gathered all the facts.* So much financial

grief could be avoided if people would only stop making major financial expenditures without really looking at all of the facts. Such blind action is downright stupid. "What a shame—yes, how stupid!—to decide before knowing the facts!" (Prov. 18:13, *TLB*). If you have not gathered all the facts, it is better to take the chance of missing the boat altogether than to jump and land in the middle of the turbulent financial waters without any boat at all!

Do not be gullible just because you are Christian. Not everyone tells the truth, and a lot of people don't tell the whole truth. So ask questions, gather facts, and check every detail. People are impoverished every day by making deals on which they failed to check all the facts before acting. "Only a simpleton believes what he is told! A prudent man checks to see where he is going" (Prov. 14:15, *TLB*).

11. Own your own home. It is a wise investment to buy your own home. There are great tax advantages. As inflation goes up, your property value goes up, and it is a great built-in way to save money, besides the personal satisfaction of owning your own home.

12. When your price is fair, do not allow someone to beat your price down. Proverbs 20:14 gives us this appropriate advice: " 'Utterly worthless!' says the buyer as he haggles over the price. But afterwards he brags about his bargain!" (*TLB*).

13. Be generous. Help those who are less fortunate than you. God hates poverty, I hate poverty, and you should hate poverty. Be the first to give compassion and love to those who are victims of poverty. "To help the poor is to honor God" (Prov. 14:31, *TLB*). The joy of having is multiplied manyfold by sharing with others.

"Happy is the generous man, the one who feeds the poor" (Prov. 22:9, *TLB*). The capping secret to a life of financial success is to share what you have with others, for it is in sharing that a man extends himself.

In helping other people, keep in mind that it is better to help a person help himself than to do it all for him. The old saying is still true, "Give a man a fish and you feed him for a day. Teach him to catch a fish and you feed him for life."

In closing this chapter on secrets of financial success, let me tell you about the all-important Abundant Life Principle. What an exciting day it was when I learned about this principle! For years I had known that Jesus came to earth to give us abundant life. Correctly I believed that this meant joy and peace, friendship and fellowship, love and fulfillment, prosperity and abundance. But my problem was that I didn't know how to activate all of this abundance into my daily living, and much of my life was anything but filled with abundance. Many people today know Jesus Christ personally but have yet to experience the abundance He wants to give them in daily living. What a joyous day it was when I received the truth of activating and using this abundant life here and now!

Here is the Abundant Life Principle that I believe is at the heart of all true financial success. In the words of Jesus,

"GIVE, AND IT SHALL BE GIVEN UNTO YOU. . . .
[DO THIS AND] YOUR GIFT WILL RETURN TO YOU
IN FULL AND OVERFLOWING MEASURE, PRESSED DOWN,
SHAKEN TOGETHER TO MAKE ROOM FOR MORE,
AND RUNNING OVER" (Luke 6:38, *KJV; TLB*).

8

HOW TO CASH IN ON TRUE RICHES

Poverty or prosperity?
Rags or riches?
Slave or master?

If the choice were yours, which would you choose? A sincere young mother asked me, "Is it wrong to want a little more out of life?" Most of us envy good fortune and prosperity. We look at those who we think have it and secretly wish we were in their shoes. Why is it that man instinctively wants to prosper? I think the answer lies in the fact that God, who is the Author of prosperity, created man in His own likeness, and that man, reflecting the very nature of the One who created him, wants to lay hold of prosperity. The truth is that *prosperity is a divine idea.*

Someone has said, "The shocking truth about prosperity is that it is shockingly right instead of shockingly wrong for you to be prosperous!"

An individual is prosperous to the extent that he is experiencing peace of mind, health, meaningful relationships, and plenty of good things in the world where he lives. I believe that a prosperous life is what God wants for you!

God Wants You to Prosper

For you God wants nothing but the best! It is God's intention for His children to reap the riches of His marvelous creation. Out of the treasure chest of the Bible comes this divine wish for you: "Beloved, I wish above all things that thou mayest prosper and be in health, even as thy soul prospereth" (3 John 2, *KJV*).

God's wish for you is, "Above all things that thou mayest prosper and be in health, even as thy soul prospereth." *Why don't you claim your inheritance?*

There is no special blessing in being poor. Obviously a person cannot be very happy if he is existing in poverty. Let's face it—poverty is a dirty, uncomfortable, degrading experience. The suffering that results from poverty is heartbreaking. "Even his own neighbors despise the poor man, while the rich have many friends" (Prov. 14:20, *TLB*). It's sure a lot better to have money than not to have it! "A poor man's own brothers turn away from him in embarrassment; how much more his friends! He calls after them, but they are gone" (Prov. 19:7, *TLB*).

God is not blessed or glorified, nor is His name honored, when He sees His creation living on less than the best. Poverty is never God's will for anyone. You are a child of the King, and a king is not glorified if he sees his son, the prince, going without the things he needs. If Jesus Christ were standing beside you this moment, I am quite sure He would not praise poverty, but He would say, "My Father is rich in houses and lands; He holds the wealth of the world in His hands. What my Father has, is yours." Prosperity is your God-given heritage.

"But whatever is good and perfect comes to us from God the Creator of all light, and he shines forever without change or shadow" (Jas. 1:17, *TLB*).

The True Riches of Life

If someone were to ask you to list the true riches of life, what would you choose to include and exclude in your list? In asking this question of several Christian friends whom I consider to have unusual wisdom and insights into life, I compiled this list of true riches:

Knowing Jesus Christ
Being with family
Having fellowship with Christian friends
Being used of God to help others
Taking time to smell the flowers
Playing with children
Achieving dreams
Overcoming obstacles
Feeling loved
Having important work to do
Sharing in conversation and
    understanding with another person
Having a close friend
Enjoying the feeling that comes
    after a good day's work
Helping another person
Breathing fresh air
Enjoying good health
Having a happy home and marriage
Having goals to achieve

Experiencing peace inside
Knowing the joy of the Lord
Having a positive attitude
Being in harmony with God and fellow
   members of the human race
Taking a walk in the woods
Possessing common sense
Being content
Having faith, hope, and love
Reading an uplifting book

After compiling this rather extensive list of the riches of life, I discovered that *not one of my friends had listed money in his list of true riches!* Thank you, Jesus, that any one of the true riches listed above can be possessed by any individual, whether or not he has money! There is no question about it—some things are worth more than money (see appendix 1, pp. 129).

The big question is, how much is money worth? One thing is sure—it is not worth as much as it used to be! On the other hand, in our affluent society today are many people to whom money means far too much. Money has become their god and master. It seems that whenever a man makes money his god, his life soon becomes filled with tragedy. Some of the saddest shipwrecks I have ever heard about have been people like Howard Hughes, who, although a billionaire, died of malnutrition and with no real friends.

In reaction to this we have the hippie culture, which avoids even the appearance of material things as society has traditionally known them. In my opinion, in over-reacting they have thrown out the baby with the bathwater. As we observe their pathetic panhandling existence, we see far more poverty than true riches.

A vivid little story I always enjoy involves two mischievous little boys who slipped through a back-alley window into the neighborhood hardware store. Cautiously they sneaked up the stairs and stepped onto the main floor of the hardware store.

Then the little urchins went to work frantically switching around all the price tags in sight. Having completed their mischief, the two boys ran back down the stairs and climbed back out through the basement window unnoticed.

Unaware of what had happened, the owner opened the store the next morning as usual. Imagine the surprise of the first customers as they discovered these astonishing prices: shiny new 10-speed bicycle, 29¢ a pound; yellow screwdriver, $39.50; big league baseball, $300.00; riding power mower with all the latest attachments, $1.95; nails, $59.00 each! Things of great value were selling for practically nothing, while things of little value had huge prices tagged on them. This is a striking picture of the way values are mixed up in the society in which you and I live today.

Keep Your Values Straight

Money does have considerable value. Many good and wonderful things can be accomplished with money. It is God who has given to you both money and the responsibility for managing it. There is no limit to how much good can be done with money that is well managed. *A faithful manager of money* is what God wants you to be. Any person who steps out of the crowd and manages his money well opens the door to the prosperous life that is our divine heritage.

About this time some of you are saying, "Now just a

minute—you've gone too far. What about the verse that Paul wrote in Timothy, 'The love of money is a root of all sorts of evil'?" (1 Tim. 6:10, *NASB*). I have no quarrel at all with the teachings of this verse. It is absolutely true that to be in love with money, to be focused emotionally on money, is to open the door to all sorts of evil. But this verse certainly does not excuse us from the responsibility of *managing* our money. Nor does it hold us back from cashing in on the abundant riches already provided for us here and now.

So let's get the record straight. There is nothing wrong with money or with wanting money. It is a God-given medium of exchange, and there is nothing evil about that. Money is a good and perfect gift that comes from God to us. But what makes money count for good or bad is our attitude toward it. How we think and feel about it can either make or break us.

Our American forefathers displayed their proper attitude toward money when they boldly printed on all our coins and currency, "In God we trust."

The Living Bible, in the book of Proverbs, puts it this way, "Trust in your money and down you go! Trust in God and flourish as a tree." In another place it says, "Greed causes fighting; trusting God leads to prosperity" (Prov. 28:25, *TLB*). A person can never have a truly prosperous life without trusting fully in God. I have noticed that a person who trusts God can weather any financial setback, any financial depression, and still come out on top. *Trust in God*, and your life will be financially happy.

Keep Your Priorities Straight

To make sure you lay hold of the riches that will fill

your life with peace, health, happiness, and abundance in your world, arrange your priorities according to God's pattern for a prosperous life.

Tim was a Christian only a few weeks when he came to me and asked how he could straighten out all the confusion in his life. On the surface it appeared that this tall striking young man and his equally attractive wife had it made in life. But the truth was that their marriage was being seriously jeopardized by financial problems caused by mixed-up priorities.

For example, Tim was playing softball four nights a week and spending little or no time at home with his wife and two children. They had two big expensive cars they were trying to keep up and yet they didn't have enough money for food and saw tithing as an impossible mountain.

I took the opportunity to explain to my new Christian friend, whom I was discipling, that we lived in a world where a lot of people had their priorities all mixed up. But in order to claim the abundant life that Jesus came to give us, it was important that we build our priorities based on scriptural truth. I further explained that often it was not a choice between what was right and wrong but between what was good, better and best. God, our heavenly Father, wants us to have the very best.

Together with Tim I wrote on a sheet of paper six words: money; God; church; family; friend; vocation. Then together we opened the Bible and aloud Tim read this important verse, "Seek ye first the kingdom of God, and His righteousness; and all these things shall be added unto you" (Matt. 6:33, *KJV*). After reading this verse together I asked Tim to arrange in order, from one to six, according to what he thought was God's order of priority for his life, the words we had already written on the paper.

After a time of intensive work and patient guidance from me, Tim's priorities read (1) God (2) family (3) church (4) friends (5) vocation and (6) money.

After Tim stared at his new list of priorities for a long time he looked up at me with a big smile of insight and said, "It sure does make a difference when you get your priorities in correct order, doesn't it?" Then he volunteered that he was going to cut his softball game down to one night a week in order to spend the needed time with his wife and children. He also made the decision to sell one of his cars and start managing his money.

In the weeks and months that followed I took great pleasure in watching this young man and his wife grow in their marriage and spiritually, as they brought their life into line with God's priorities and continued to follow His pattern for successful living. Putting God first in their lives, and putting each other next, surely did pay rich dividends for this young couple.

Many single women have a rather difficult time supporting themselves financially. By the time they pay their rent and possibly a car payment and a few other important items, there is not too much left.

Janet White is a single person who loves Jesus and endeavors to put God first in everything she does. Last year, in order to cut down her expenses, she accepted the generous offer of a family to live with them at greatly reduced rent. The lady of the house and Janet became close friends. One evening, when the benefactor was trying to show Janet how to economize, she firmly suggested that Janet must no longer tithe to her church, but should reduce her giving to around a dollar a week.

Feeling the pressure from this woman who had been so good to her, Janet came to a Thursday night Bible study group, and, in the openness of Christian fellowhip, shared her pressing problem. In responsive love the group prayed that Janet might have the courage to put God first, in spite of the possible displeasure of her friends.

The following day Janet took on new courage and seized the opportunity to witness to the well-meaning friend that God had to come first in her financial life. She explained that she did not expect her friend to understand this, but asked her to respect it. And the friend didn't understand, but she did respect Janet for her strong faith in action. Don't you forget it—every time we put God first we bear a true witness.

Eight months later, in the same Bible study fellowship, Janet reported that she had received two very substantial raises and had been promoted to one of the highest positions she could achieve at that time in her career—all since the time she stood up and put God first. Janet is praising God for His wonderful doings and because He keeps His promise. "In everything you do, put God first, and he will direct you and crown your efforts with success" (Prov. 3:6, *TLB*).

Your number one key for a more prosperous life is to make God number one in all you do.

Cash in on Contentment

Inflation . . . cost of living up . . . stock market going down . . . price rip-offs . . . world food shortage. Yes, it's true, as you know all too well, that our dollar buys less and less. But the truth that the negative headlines do not tell us is that we Americans *still have more than any people who have ever lived.* It is time to be thankful. Stand up and refuse to be depressed by the negative press!

Isn't it strange that there is so much discontentment among people who have so much. On the other hand, this is not surprising when we stop to consider that advertisers spend billions of dollars annually to sow the seeds of discontent within all of us. Hundreds of times throughout an average day through television, radio, newspapers, magazines, billboards, and catalogs we are cleverly enticed to look at what we *don't have* instead of what we *do have.*

Recently a young mother told me how she restored contentment to her own mind and heart—she stopped looking through catalogs and thinking about all the things she didn't have. If going shopping makes you discontented with what you have and makes you want to buy things you can't afford, then the answer is to simply stop shopping.

To enrich your life with contentment, close the door on discontent by refusing to focus on what you don't have. Like Paul, whether in prison or out of prison, in hunger or in plenty, you can learn to say, "For I have learned, in whatsoever state I am, therewith to be content" (Phil. 4:11, *KJV*). As Bill Gothard, head of the Institute in Basic Youth Conflicts, puts it, "Contentment is realizing that God has provided everything I need for my present circumstances."

To cash in on contentment here are five positive things to do:

1. Count your blessings. Think over the good things in your life, the things the Lord has done for you. Write down 10 things you are thankful for.

Look at the loaf, not the crumbs. This old story bears telling once again. As the baker's cart jostled down the narrow street, a loaf of bread fell to the cobblestones. Quickly the sparrows from under the eaves of the nearby houses scrambled to fight over the crumbs which had broken off the loaf. When the crumbs were gone the birds flew off, leaving the loaf itself untouched.

So it is with the critic. Pouncing on the crumbs, he overlooks the loaf. Lesson: *Don't be a birdbrain,* seeing only the crumbs in our world!

2. *Pause to enjoy what God has given you.* Little things light up life with sunshine. Open your eyes to see romance in the commonplace. One of my favorite experiences is to arrive home after a long day, get down on the floor, and play with toddler Ann. One of our fun games is peekaboo. How we enjoy laughing at each other and with each other! How about it? Are you taking time to enjoy what you already have?

3. *Try being thankful for yourself.* You are indeed a person worth being thankful for. You aren't perfect, but there is surely a lot of good in you. Be thankful for yourself as a human being whom God loves and whom He wants you to love. You are uniquely created by God—there is no one else like you.

4. *Start thanking God for the difficult.* Some of the greatest helps to rich living given in the Bible are the hardest to swallow. Take this one: "In everything give thanks: for this is the will of God in Christ Jesus concerning you" (1 Thess. 5:18, *KJV*). Again and again you find the word "Rejoice!" in the Bible. The psalmist continually spoke of joy in the midst of trouble. "Thou hast turned for me my mourning into dancing," says David (Ps. 30:11, *KJV*).

103

You mean we are to give thanks in hardships?
Yes.
When misunderstood?
Yes.
When taken advantage of?
Yes.
In everything give thanks.

Dear brothers, is your life full of money difficulties? "Then be happy, for when the way is rough, your patience has a chance to grow" (Jas. 1:2,3 *TLB*). Difficulties develop character, give a person a chance to expand and grow. As someone has said so unforgettably, "Bloom where you are planted."

The bigger your money problems, the greater your challenge. What a man is like when things go dead against him—that is the test! The last 10 feet of the race, the last 30 seconds of the game, the last bell in the fight—these things can make the man. When the going gets tough, the tough get going. No matter what financial hardships you face, *thank the Lord.*

5. *Share what you have with others.* To be rich in contentment, multiply your blessing by giving joyfully to others.

One Sunday night in our evening fellowship service, some real edification took place. My wife described how at Thanksgiving time, in response to my encouraging people to write letters of thanksgiving and appreciation to someone who meant a lot to them, she had written a letter of appreciation and thanks to a high school band teacher whom she had not seen for at least 10 years. Before she could change her mind she mailed the letter, then for weeks wondered if she had done the right thing. In the midst of Christmas cards came a beautiful reply.

Not only had her band teacher received the letter, but this is what he said it did for him:

Dear Margi and Family,
What a pleasant surprise to receive your letter at Thanksgiving. It made me feel like I was "King for a Day." Thanks, I needed that!

As Margi related this happy experience her face radiated with gladness and we were all made happier. There is nothing like an expression of thanks to multiply and spread happiness in every direction. Positive emotions, expressed openly, never fail to build self-esteem and recharge the psychic battery of both the giver and the receiver.

For a great lifter-upper, join the happiness experiment. In some way, before this very day ends, express your love, appreciation, and thanks to another person. You select the method—write a letter, pick up the phone, send a gift, or visit someone face-to-face. *To be rich in contentment, give happiness away.*

WHERE LOVE AND THANKS ARE GIVEN AWAY,
GOD IS.
WHERE GOD IS,
THERE ARE HIS CHILDREN
CASHING IN ON TRUE RICHES.

9
OPEN YOUR DOOR TO UNLIMITED SUPPLY

What a breathtaking, awe-inspiring, overwhelming view. There it was—the tall, snow-capped mountain standing like a ruling giant in the background. Beneath the mountain were open green meadows surrounded by towering fir trees. And there, flowing 5 feet deep from rocks 30 feet across, was the sparkling Metolius River.

They tell us that this abundant flow of water coming out of the rocks never stops. From where this unlimited supply comes the scientists can only guess. What a mind-expanding sight, created by a God who knows no limit!

As I stood there in the middle of scenic Oregon, beholding one of the wonders of the world, I thought about how this everflowing water bears witness to our God of unlimited supply.

This week as I was meditating on some of my personal needs and the needs that we have as a church, the Holy Spirit brought this great verse to my heart and mind:

107

"Now glory be to God who by his mighty power at work within us is able to do far more than we would ever dare to ask or even dream of—infinitely beyond our highest prayers, desires, thoughts, or hopes" (Eph. 3:20, *TLB*).

Make God Your Source of Supply

There is no limit of supply with God. I grew up in an affluent generation, in which we took our natural resources for granted. It came as a real shock to me to learn that we are depleting many of our natural resources. They tell us that in the years ahead we can expect to run out of such vital resources as natural gas and oil. But before we panic over this energy crisis, let us look to the One who created us all in the first place—God.

I believe God has ways of providing for our energy needs that our scientists haven't yet even dreamed of. There is no limit to what God has done to supply our needs in the past, and there is no limit to what He can do to supply our needs in the future. Neither is there any limit to what He will do to supply our need in the *now* if we will look to Him for the answer.

There is no question more crucial to the solution of your money problems than this one: *Who is your source?* If your employer is your source, you are going to be disappointed. If your attention is on things you can't afford to buy, you are in for double trouble. If you are trusting in your own cleverness to get you out of this situation, then you are in for some depressing days ahead. If you are looking to another person to supply your needs, you are going to go without. But if you look to God He will neither disappoint you nor let you down.

Put God first. Make God your source, and succeed in

solving the financial problems in your life. I believe the Bible when it promises, "In everything you do, put God first, and he will direct you and crown your efforts with success" (Prov. 3:6, *TLB*).

Do you want financial success? *Then put God first in all your money decisions.*

Do you want the best things in life? *Then give God your best.*

It is not what is your source but Who is your Source that will make the difference. Every time I take my eyes off Jesus and start looking to my own genius or to another person to supply either my personal needs or the needs of our church, it doesn't happen. But when I look to Jesus as my Lord and Provider, I am provided for in abundance. You do believe the Bible, don't you? Then believe it when God promises you this: "But my God shall supply all your needs according to his riches in glory by Christ Jesus" (Phil. 4:19, *KJV*). Thank you, Jesus, for supplying all my needs and more!

Don't limit God. Jesus said, "You have not because you ask not." If you are not receiving an abundance of good things in your life, the chances are it is because in some way you are limiting God. It is the most natural thing in the world for the abundant supply of good things to flow from God into your life. It is His desire for you. How do people limit God?

- by withholding what God wants;
- by trying to live life their own way;
- by not really believing what the Bible says about God wanting them to prosper;
- by thinking too small or too little;
- by not putting God first;
- by failing to give seed faith.

People who are on a small or limited income often feel they cannot afford to give or share. But by *not* giving they stop their own receiving of a greater supply, because they are violating the biblical principle of giving and receiving. They have not yet learned the secret of unlimited supply pointed out by Solomon: "It is possible to give away and become richer! It is also possible to hold on too tightly and lose everything" (Prov. 11:24, *TLB*).

Take the lid off your mind. Have you heard the story of the jumping fleas? There were at least 10,000 fleas spread like a blanket across the teacher's desk. To entertain themselves they started playing a rather wild game called the jumping game. Higher and higher they jumped, again and again, trying to outjump all the other fleas.

Then it happened! The killjoy teacher sneaked up on them and covered them with a jar. Not knowing what had happened, they kept hitting their heads on the top of the jar as they jumped up and down. But after being battered on the head a few times, they got the message and stopped jumping so high. After that they would still jump, but would stop an inch from the top of the jar. After an hour the teacher removed the jar, but those fleas never knew the difference, because, now in their minds, they had fixed an imaginary ceiling. Although the jar was removed, they refused ever again to try to jump any higher than the self-imposed ceilings that they had set in their minds.

I want to let you in on a very important secret. I call this *the secret of unlimited supply.* You must be careful not to cut off the flow of supply that God wants to give you by thinking it has to come in a certain way (for example, through a fixed income). What I want you to see is that when you make God your Source, He has infinite avenues of bringing the right supply to meet your need. Don't be surprised if your supply comes through unexpected channels and in unexpected ways. Such are the ways of an unlimited God.

Sow Good Seeds and Reap Rich Benefits

Before moving to the Northwest and settling down in Portland, I was pastor of a church in the middle of the Midwest, located in Lawrence, Kansas. Surrounding Lawrence are huge wheat farms scattered throughout the countryside. In the springtime, when driving down the country roads on the way to visit parishioners, it was a breathtaking experience to look out across those golden wheat fields standing on the verge of another golden bumper harvest. How did such a beautiful harvest of grain come to be? One thing is for sure—it didn't just happen. Months before, in the fall of the year, the farmers went out and toiled in their fields to prepare the soil; then, with full expectation of a harvest, they planted the seed. It is the law written in nature—planting time is followed by harvest time. Before you can expect the harvest you must first plant the seed.

Last summer I saw a nine-year-old boy standing in awe as he stared up into the heights of a towering oak tree. Who doesn't admire a tall, mighty oak tree? No doubt the boy was wondering where the oak came from, with all of its splendor and enormous strength. Did it just happen to be? No! Many years before a tiny seed was sown. There can be no tall oak tree without first the sowing of a seed. There are enormous potential and possibilities in one tiny seed when it has been activated

111

by being sown. Sow a seed and you activate vast powers far beyond your own.

So many people are living without, simply because they are not properly making use of the law of sowing and reaping. It is to your utmost benefit to learn and make good use of the law of sowing and reaping, for as the Bible says, "For whatsoever man soweth, that shall he also reap" (Gal. 6:7, *KJV*). How you use this law will determine what you reap in your life. If you sow good seed you will reap a return of rich rewards. On the other hand, if you sow bad seed you will reap a bad return.

Right now stop sowing bad seeds like these:

When we buy things we cannot afford now,
    saying, "I'll pay later."
When we spend more money than we make.
When we borrow at high rates of interest.
When we spend every cent we make and more.
When we fail to plan for emergencies.
When we neglect to buy proper insurance.
When we borrow money to buy
    everyday essentials.
When we sign a note with someone else.
When we fall for get-rich-quick schemes.
When we begin to think someone is going
    to give us something for nothing.
When we start writing checks
    before we have the money.
When we go to the grocery store without a list.
When we don't shop for the best price.
When we buy things we don't need.

Sow good seeds and reap rich benefits. Start right today, taking full advantage of the law of sowing and reaping by planting nothing but good seeds. If you willfully and intentionally sow good seeds you are going to reap a most glorious return.

The Bible says this about a man: "If he plants the good things of the Spirit, he will reap the everlasting life which the Holy Spirit gives him" (Gal. 6:8, *TLB*). As long as a man has breath it is never too late for him to start sowing good seeds. Have you been sowing some good seeds? Then sow more good seeds for a more prosperous life. To cash in on the good things, sow good seeds like these:

Sow pure thoughts, reap clean actions.
Sow friendship, reap friends.
Sow positive thinking, reap a positive life.
Sow prayers, reap answers.
Sow love, reap more love.
Sow kindness, reap gratitude.
Sow hard work, reap promotions.
Sow commitment to Jesus Christ, reap
*   eternal benefits and life everlasting.*

Plant Seed-Faith at the Point of Your Need

The most potent thing in nature is one of the tiniest—the seed. Within every seed there lie explosive possibilities. One little seed planted in the earth can bring forth enough food to feed many people.

In the spiritual world there is nothing more powerful than faith. Jesus spoke of this unmatched power when He said, "Verily I say unto you, If ye have faith as a grain of mustard seed, ye shall say unto this mountain, Remove hence to yonder place; and it shall remove: and nothing shall be impossible unto you" (Matt. 17:20, *KJV*).

When you put seed and faith together, you join the

most powerful of both natural and supernatural forces to provide you with unlimited supply. Whatever seed you give in faith, God Himself will multiply back to you manyfold.

What is seed-faith? Seed-faith is something you put yourself into and give in the name of Jesus. It may be your time or your friendship; it can be service rendered or a prayer offered; it can be money you give to God. The greater the sacrifice, the bigger the seed. The bigger the seed you plant, the more potential for receiving a multiplied return.

A tithe is not a debt we owe but a seed we sow. Just this week my secretary was telling me how her income is one-third of what it was when she was married, but that all this year she has still tithed to the Lord first. Before, with two-thirds more income, there was never enough money to go around, but now there is actually some money left over after the bills are paid!

I'm going to tell you something that makes no logical sense. An accountant would throw up his hands and say this is horrible teaching. It just doesn't add up at the end of the pencil, but here it is anyway: I believe with all my heart that when a person is in financial difficulty, the very first step for getting out from under depressing debts is to put God first by tithing. You see, tithing is *not a debt you owe but a seed you sow.* It is a seed that unlocks the door to greater supply in your life.

The Scriptures teach us this very pointed lesson: While the children of Israel tithed to the Lord they prospered, but whenever they withheld the tithe from the Lord hardships came upon them.

God said, "Bring ye all the tithes into the storehouse, that there may be meat in mine house, and prove me

114

now herewith, saith the Lord of Hosts, if I will not open you the windows of heaven, and pour you out a blessing, that there shall not be room enough to receive it" (Mal. 3:10, *KJV*). And I believe it. *God loves to bless and prosper His people.*

What you give is what you get. When you sow a seed by giving, you give God something to work with. On the other hand, if you give nothing—nothing times nothing is nothing! If only you can grasp the truth of this great promise God has for you: "For if you give, you will get! Your gift will return to you in full and overflowing measure, pressed down, shaken together to make room for more, and running over" (Luke 6:38, *TLB*).

Do you have financial needs in your life today? Do you need additional supply in your life? Then give God something to work with, so that He might meet your need. Let's suppose a farmer had 100 bushels of grain. He plants 10 bushels of seeds in the fields and leaves 90 bushels in the barn. The seed left in the barn cannot produce anything; it is the seed *planted in the field* that goes into action to make the harvest. It is only *what we give God* that He multiplies. It is *not what we keep. Give first, and you will receive a landslide return later.*

Tom had been a Christian for only two months when he asked, "Pastor, how much should I give every week to the Lord's work?" I said, "That's a good question." (Wherever the tithe is talked about in a group, someone will always ask, "Are we to pay the tithe on what we make *before* taxes or *after* taxes are deducted?" That is another good question.)

I answered my young convert by first asking him these questions: How much do you want to make? How much do you want God to prosper your life? How much do you covet God's blessings upon your family, upon your total life? I said, "Let's suppose you give God nothing. Nothing multiplied by nothing equals zero. On the other hand, you can give God something and get an increased amount back. You see, whatever you give God is going to increase, so how much do you want to give?"

Have you heard about the law of proportionate return? The Scriptures teach us, "Whatever measure you use to give—large or small—will be used to measure what is given back to you" (Luke 6:38, *TLB*). Do you want only a little? Then give only a little. Do you want a lot? Then give a lot. Your return will be in direct proportion to how much you sow. The Bible says in another place, "But this I say, He which soweth sparingly shall reap also sparingly; and he which soweth bountifully shall reap also bountifully" (2 Cor. 9:6, *KJV*).

Even as you read this today you have a need in your life. Your particular need may be small or it may be large. Your financial problems may be few or they may be many. Whatever your need, whatever the magnitude of your problems, you can do something about them, starting right now. Give seed-faith at the point of your need. The greater the need, the bigger the seed you need to plant in faith.

Just months before starting New Hope Community Church I had mountains of need in my life. I was a pastor of 10 years without a place to preach and without any financial support, and, worse yet, with no prospects of support. We needed friends. We needed a ministry. We needed a job. We needed income. What could we do?

We sold our house, took the $6,000 that we netted

from the sale, and planted one huge portion of seed-faith in the beginning of New Hope Community Church. It was without a doubt a big sacrificial gift that we gave. It represented all that Margi and I had in the way of material possessions in the world. But we had an enormous need, and the seed-faith had to match that need.

Where can I begin to tell you of how that one seed-faith opened up God's unlimited supply in our life. To us He has given beautiful close friends, a ministry of hope and healing that is now reaching into the thousands and expanding daily, and a four-bedroom home with a garden setting that we enjoy together and with many friends. *Give at the point of your need, and you too will receive.*

Expect a landslide return. The widow of Zarephath was financially poor. She lived in a day when conditions were terrible, with famine and drought throughout the land. Every day people were dying from starvation. Yet when Elijah, visiting man of God, asked her to prepare him a cake, she used her last handful of meal and last cup of oil. This generous lady gave all she had! How easy it would have been for her to say, "I'm sorry, Elijah, but I am awfully hard up; I need the food for my own family. Besides, charity begins at home, you know."

How fortunate it was for this woman that she had the courage to go ahead and give anyway! If she had held back, refusing to feed Elijah, she would have been sowing seeds of starvation. She would have saved the fuel and the oil, only to lose it in the long run. What we grasp too tightly we lose. Because the widow dared to sow seed-faith, tremendous things happened as a result (see 1 Kings 17:8–16).

Make God your source of supply; plant seed-faith at

the point of your need, and you can expect a landslide return.

All of us have observed on a product words to the effect, "If not pleased, money back guaranteed." Have you ever tried to collect on one of those deals? It isn't easy! They say it, but not many companies do it. But with God you can count on His money-back guarantee. Not only does He give you back everything you give in faith, but He multiplies it manyfold.

Unfortunately, some Christians don't use all the good sense God has given them. They act like the retarded boy who tried to farm. Each year he would plant the seed, but he never bothered to look for the harvest, let alone harvest it. For a long time in my Christian life I tithed, but what an exciting day when I learned about seed-faith—that I could give in faith and expect a return of unlimited supply.

There is no way you can outgive God. "Thank God for His Son—His Gift too wonderful for words" (2 Cor. 9:15, *TLB*). God gave it all when He gave us Jesus, but He doesn't stop there. In response to our giving back to Him, He gives all the more. He gives first, He gives second, and every time we give He gives more and more! "For God, who gives seed to the farmer to plant, and later on, good crops to harvest and eat, will give you more and more seed to plant and will make it grow so that you can give away more and more fruit from your harvest" (2 Cor. 9:10, *TLB*). *God multiplies and gives the increase to the giver.*

If you were to take $1,000 and put it in one of our local banks, you could expect to draw 6 percent interest on it annually. At the end of the first year it would have increased by $60 to the amount of $1,060.

But let's suppose you take that same $1,000 and give it as seed-faith to God. What is given in seed-faith God multiplies two times, or four times, or 10 times, or sometimes, the Scriptures tell us even 100 times. Instead of having $1,000 for the year you could find yourself receiving $10,000 or $20,000 or even $100,000! Seed-faith is the most potent power of all the seeds. Use it, and it will open your door to an unlimited supply.

THANK YOU, JESUS,
THAT THE DOORS OF UNLIMITED SUPPLY
ARE SWINGING WIDE OPEN.
"GIVE AND YOU SHALL RECEIVE!"

10

MOVE AHEAD AND GAIN FINANCIAL FREEDOM

I have written this book because I believe with all my heart that Jesus came to give us life more abundantly beginning here and now. Too many times I've seen good people bogged down in the mire of financial debt to the point where all the joy in their life is gone. So much human suffering resulting from mismanagement can be and will be overcome as God's children begin practicing biblical teaching on finances. Becoming a good steward of what God has given us is a very important part of our Christian witness.

I firmly believe that there are no money problems that do not have solutions. The solutions are to be found, first of all, in developing the right attitude and perspective toward money itself. Second, we must practice the biblical principles of finance. Third, we must deny the less to gain the greater, and, most important of all, we must put God first in all that we do in money matters.

What matters is not where you are financially, but where, with God's help, you are going. To be a Christian is not to be without problems, but it is to *face problems*, to *learn from mistakes*, and to *rise up and overcome* by turning mountainous problems into mountainous successes.

Not only are you going to find solutions to your money problems, but, as you make application of the truths in this book, you are going to have this marvelous promise fulfilled in your life: "Beloved, I wish above all things that thou mayest prosper and be in health, even as thy soul prospereth" (3 John 2, *KJV*).

Five Steps to Financial Advancement

1. Visualize exactly where you want to go financially. When people are in the midst of money problems they get to the desperation point, where all they can see are the problems. Immediate money problems are symptoms of a need for long-range money planning. If things are to be different a year from now, three years from now, five years from now, you must see beyond the immediate problems to the goal which, with God's help you intend to reach financially.

Remember, things that look impossible now can actually become a reality five years from now, or 10 years from now, or perhaps 20 years from now if you decide where it is you want to go and get moving in that direction. One step forward, followed by another, and then another, can in time get you to places you never dreamed possible. It is amazing what can be accomplished over a given period of time if you set your sight on a goal and keep moving toward that achievement.

2. *Work your plan.* Someone has said that God is a God of order, not of confusion. One of the things I have emphasized throughout this entire book is that for a person's financial picture to clear up and confusion to end, one must accept and follow God's guidelines for financial success. Our God-given responsibility in the area of finances is to become the manager of our money.

Throughout this book the word *plan* stands out. The older I become the more I am seeing the truth of the statement, *When you fail to plan, you plan to fail.* You could spend no more valuable time than planning where you want to go financially, then writing on paper how you plan to get there step-by-step.

I think the first step anyone should take in good financial planning is to plan to sow the seed-faith of being a tither.

On New Year's Day of this year God gave me this promise verse: "In everything you do, put God first, and he will direct you and crown your efforts with success" (Prov. 3:6, *TLB*). I believe this verse because I have been practicing it in my life and experiencing some real crowning successes. The simple truth is that if you are to enjoy God's blessing financially, you must put Him first and foremost in all your financial plans.

In doing wise financial planning, the second step to take is this: Map out a plan for eliminating all depressing debt that is owed on depreciating items.

The third thing that a sound financial plan should include is a preplanned way of saving something out of every dollar that is made.

3. *Commit yourself to the task of moving ahead financially.* Multitudes of people simply drift through

life, failing to accomplish much of anything simply because they are uncommitted to anything. They are a little like the man who discovered that his dog had fleas, so since he didn't have any commitment to the dog, he simply shot the dog and bought a new dog. The only problem was, when he got home guess what he discovered? His new dog had fleas too! How much simpler it would have been to correct the flea problem instead of getting rid of the dog. If you have money problems, no matter how you try to excuse it, there is only one way to solve your problems: With God's help dig in and manage your money.

To do this means commitment. Let me tell you that it is the *commitments* in my life that bring me the best. All the good things that have flowed into my life have come as a result of my commitment to Jesus. My commitment to my wife, Margi, for better or for worse fills my life with a warm, sharing, caring relationship. What would our marriage be without commitment? To get anything good in life takes commitment. And to get ahead financially and to come out on top of problems, like depressing debt, takes real commitment. You do want to solve your money problems, don't you? Then in the name of Jesus commit yourself to managing your money. Make this great verse your motto: "I can do all things through Christ which strengtheneth me" (Phil. 4:13, *KJV*).

4. *Begin right now, where you are this day, to manage your money.* There will never be a better day to start than today. Tomorrow will never be any different; it will just have the same old money problems unless you decide to begin to manage *now!*

5. *Deny the lesser to gain the greater.* Do you want

to achieve the financial stability, plus surplus, that is the desire of your heart? It is going to cost you something. It seems that everybody wants something for nothing, and this is especially true in the area of finance. But life doesn't give good things for nothing; for nothing you get nothing.

To get the best things in life there is a price to be paid. In the 1976 Olympic Games held in Montreal, it was indeed a moment to cheer when 26-year-old Bruce Jenner won the grueling 10-day decathlon competition and was acclaimed "the world's greatest athlete."

This moment of personal victory and world tribute did not come easily. Jenner had trained long and hard for the decathlon after finishing ninth in 1972 at Munich. It was reported by sports writers that he trained with nonstop dedication for more than seven hours a day for four years. Think of what this young man denied himself in order to become the world's greatest athlete! The Bible says it this way: "To win the contest you must deny yourselves many things that would keep you from doing your best" (1 Cor. 9:25, *TLB*).

Yes, there is a price to be paid for winning financially. The question you must now ask yourself is this: Is it worth the effort to go without, to say no, to tell your loved ones you can't afford some things? Is it worth these things to solve your financial problems?

You cannot have the greater financially unless you are first willing to deny the lesser. I'm sorry, but there is no other way. You can read all the books in the world, but the bare fact is that you must pay the price of self-discipline to overcome and become financially free.

Is it worth the effort? Scores of people with whom I have worked for the past several years are saying after one year or two years or three years that all the hard work of money management is well worth the effort. When on paydays someone else doesn't take all your money—when you've got money left over—it's worth it! When there is harmony in the family instead of tension and misunderstanding over money, you had better believe it's worth it!

It's All in Your Hands

The young know-it-all just home from college challenged the wise old man of the mountain, "Old man, ever since I was a little boy I've heard it said that you are the wisest man in all these parts. Tell me now, is this bird that I hold in my hand dead or is it alive?"

Even as the young man in his know-it-all voice said these words, he held up his hands that were clutched together containing the bird. It was his preplanned scheme to show up the old man by proving to all the villagers that he was now smarter than their hero. His plan was this: If the old man said the bird was dead, he would open his hands and set the bird free. On the other hand, if the old man chose to say the bird was alive, he would squeeze his hands together and kill the bird. Either way, the old man was sure to be wrong, and the young man would become known as the smartest man in mountain country.

But the boy did not calculate on the wisdom of years. To the boy's challenge, "Is this bird dead or alive?" the old man calmly placed the responsibility right back on the young man's shoulders with the words, "Young man, the precious life of the bird is in your hands. The final decision as to whether the bird will die or live is yours alone to make."

As the cost of living skyrockets and inflation runs amuck, truly, your finances are like that fragile bird. The decision as to what you will do with the truths we have shared together in this book is now in your hands.

NOW MOVE AHEAD
BY DENYING THE LESSER
TO GAIN THE GREATER:
WITH GOD'S HELP YOU WILL NOT ONLY
SOLVE ALL YOUR FINANCIAL PROBLEMS,
BUT YOU WILL GAIN
FINANCIAL FREEDOM.

THESE THINGS ARE WORTH MORE THAN MONEY

1. Knowing God is more important. Knowing God is basic to all other knowledge, for the Bible says, "For the reverence and fear of God are basic to all wisdom. Knowing God results in every other kind of understanding" (Prov. 9:10, *TLB*).

2. Respect for the Lord is more important. "True humility and respect for the Lord lead a man to riches, honor and long life" (Prov. 22:4, *TLB*).

3. Righteousness, which comes from being in a right relationship with God, is more important. "Your riches won't help you on Judgment Day; only righteousness counts then" (Prov. 11:4, *TLB*).

4. Obeying God's laws and principles is more important. "God doesn't listen to the prayers of men who flout the law" (Prov. 28:9, *TLB*).

5. *Good relationships with other people are more important.* "People curse the man who holds his grain for higher prices, but they bless the man who sells it to them in time of need" (Prov. 11:26, *TLB*).

6. *Kindness is more important.* "Honor goes to kind and gracious women, mere money to cruel men. Your own soul is nourished when you are kind; it is destroyed when you are cruel" (Prov. 11:16,17, *TLB*).

7. *To be wise is more important.* "Wisdom is a tree of life to those who eat her fruit; happy is the man who keeps on eating it" (Prov. 3:18, *TLB*).

8. *Finding out what is right and doing it is more important.* "The man who knows right from wrong and has good judgment and common sense is happier than the man who is immensely rich!" (Prov. 3:13,14, *TLB*).

9. *Having God's blessing is more important.* "The good shall never lose God's blessings, but the wicked shall lose everything" (Prov. 10:30, *TLB*).

10. *Good sense is far more important.* "Good sense is far more valuable than gold or precious jewels" (Prov. 20:15, *TLB*).

11. *A good name is more important.* "If you must choose, take a good name rather than great riches; for to be held in loving esteem is better than silver and gold" (Prov. 22:1, *TLB*).

12. *To be fair in our dealing with the less fortunate is more important.* "Income from exploiting the poor will end up in the hands of someone who pities them" (Prov. 28:8, *TLB*).

13. *A humble spirit is worth more than great riches.* "Pride goes before destruction and haughtiness before a fall. Better poor and humble than proud and rich" (Prov. 16:18,19, *TLB*). "The rich man thinks of his wealth as

an impregnable defense, a high wall of safety. What a dreamer!" (Prov. 18:11, *TLB*).

14. Honesty is more important. "Ill-gotten gain brings no lasting happiness; right living does" (Prov. 10:2, *TLB*). "It is better to be poor than dishonest" (Prov. 19:22, *TLB*). "The Lord despises every kind of cheating" (Prov. 20:10 *TLB*). "Better be poor and honest than rich and dishonest" (Prov. 19:1, *TLB*). "Some men enjoy cheating, but the cake they buy with such ill-gotten gain will turn to gravel in their mouths" (Prov. 20:17, *TLB*). "Dishonest gain will never last, so why take the risk?" (Prov. 21:6, *TLB*). "Better to be poor and honest then rich and a cheater" (Prov. 28:6, *TLB*). "Dishonest money brings grief to all the family, but hating bribes brings happiness" (Prov. 15:27, *TLB*). "A little, gained honestly, is better than great wealth gotten by dishonest means" (Prov. 16:8, *TLB*).

15. Fairness is more important than financial gain. "The Lord demands fairness in every business deal. He established this principle" (Prov. 16:11, *TLB*).

HAVING WISDOM
IS MORE IMPORTANT THAN HAVING MONEY.

HOW TO STRETCH YOUR DOLLARS

How to Save Money on Food

1. Never go to the grocery store when you are hungry.
2. Make use of prepared shopping lists.
3. Make cost comparisons between different sizes and brands, and save by making the best purchases.
4. Look through the newspaper ads for the best buys and take advantage of the food sales.
5. Earn a double savings and add to your real income without increasing taxes by raising your own garden; make our own food bank by canning and freezing vegetables from the garden.
6. Use plastic bags for garbage, food covers, and lunch bags.
7. Save aluminum foil and reuse it.

8. Clip and save coupons and make use of them in shopping.

9. Do grocery shopping on sale days.

10. Buy products wholesale from farmers at the peak of the growing season, and can and freeze them.

11. Buy bread and baked goods from bakery thrift outlets.

12. Save margarine wrappers and use them to grease baked potatoes and cookie sheets.

13. Stay away from expensive pre-prepared foods.

14. Stock up on sale items. Do this consistently.

15. Brown-bag it. Take a lunch to school or to work instead of eating out.

16. Buy your meat in large quantities.

17. For snacks, give children carrots, celery, other fresh vegetables, or different kinds of fruits. Not only will it save money, but it will be a better diet for them.

18. Eat at home regularly; eat at restaurants only for special treats.

19. Plan menus as far ahead as possible and do most of your shopping in one regular trip.

20. Instead of buying canned or bottled soft drinks, mix powdered drinks at home.

21. Mix soybean into your meat to make it go further.

22. Mix reconstituted powdered milk with regular milk.

23. Buy house brands rather than nationally advertised brands. They are invariably cheaper and often of comparable quality. In many instances, the house brands are actually canned by the same firm, except under different labels.

How to Save Money on Medical Expenses

24. Practice preventive medicine.

25. Get children's inoculations at your county health department.
26. Get dental work done at a local dental school.
27. Make sure that you carry adequate medical insurance, including major medical coverage.

How to Save Money when Buying or Selling a House
28. Sell your own home, using a local title company for closing procedures, and thereby save the realtor's fee.
29. When selling your home, try to find a buyer who will assume your present loan, thereby eliminating the payoff penalty.
30. By buying a new home, you can eliminate a larger portion of advanced tax reserves needed to get you into the home.
31. When buying a home, shop around for the lowest possible interest rate.
32. Before purchasing a home, have experts check the home thoroughly in every aspect.

How to Save Money on Your Telephone Bill
33. Use direct dialing.
34. Try to place your phone calls on weekends or at night, when the rate is cheaper.
35. Phone station-to-station by prearranged appointments.
36. Time your calls and limit yourself.
37. Write letters whenever possible instead of calling long distance.

How to Save Money on Clothes
38. Sew your own clothes.
39. In buying children's clothing, shop for clothes in

which the seams are cut wide enough to allow you to let them out.

40. Buy your clothes on sale.

41. Trade children's clothes with friends.

42. Buy clothes at reduced prices through catalogs, sales, secondhand shops, swap meets, and garage sales. Nickels and dimes do matter. After a while they do mount up!

How to Save Money on Your Vacation

43. Camp along the way and save hotel costs.

44. When traveling, eat your noon meal in the car or at picnic sites.

How to Save Money on Your Car

45. The best way to save gas is not to use it at all.

46. When you start your car, go somewhere.

47. Drive nice and easy, even when traffic isn't.

48. Slow and steady driving saves.

49. Be nice to your car—keep it tuned up and in good repair.

50. Ride with someone else. Lots of money can be saved by going places together.

51. Drive an economy car. Take a look at this mileage cost comparison: At 15 mpg, 60¢ a gallon, 1,000 miles, you pay $40.00. At 30 mpg, 60¢ a gallon, 1,000 miles, you pay $20.00. During 15,000 miles in one year an economy car could save you as much as $300!

52. Purchase your oil and filter from a discount store and change your own oil.

53. Consider buying a late-model used car instead of a brand-new one, thereby eliminating the first year of heavy depreciation.

54. Keep your car an extra year—everyone knows the value of a car depreciates fastest when it's new. It follows, therefore, that your yearly depreciation diminishes each year you keep the same car.

55. If you have a mechanic friend, you might do some kind of work for him in return for free mechanical work.

56. When purchasing a car, you should be able to obtain a lower interest rate at a local bank with at least one-third of the down payment.

57. When trading cars, sell your own car by advertising in the newspaper.

58. When buying a car, decide exactly what you want and shop for the right price.

59. Plan errands and do several things at a time when you make a trip to town.

How to Save Money on Your Home Energy

60. Use small appliances in place of major appliances; note tips on preparing dishes that you might think are only possible in an oven or on a range.

61. Read the recipe booklets that often come with small appliances; note tips on preparing dishes that you might think are only possible in an oven or on a range.

62. Change the bag on your vacuum cleaner frequently to make your cleaner more efficient.

63. Turn off your radio, television, and stereo when you are not listening.

64. If buying a new TV set, look for solid-state types—they use less energy.

65. Keep appliances in top shape so they won't waste energy.

66. Set water-heater thermostat lower.

67. **Repair leaky hot-water faucets immediately.**

68. Taking showers instead of baths can save up to half of the total hot water used in a household.

69. If away from home for more than three days, turn off the water heater.

70. Turn off lights in a room when no one is there.

71. Use lower wattage bulbs in areas where lower lighting levels can be used, such as closets and hallways.

72. Automatic timers are available which turn lights on and off at prescribed intervals. This can help to discourage crime and can cut down the cost of having lights on continually.

73. When washing, adjust water levels for partial loads or else make sure you wash with full loads.

74. Avoid wasting hot water while laundering.

75. Keep the lint filter clean on your dryer, thereby saving energy.

76. Iron large amounts of clothing at one time to avoid heating up an iron several times a day or week.

77. Make sure that the insulation in your ceilings, walls, and flooring is adequate, in order to cut down on heating costs.

78. Install storm windows or double-pane glass for doors and windows in order to cut down on heat losses.

79. Clean or replace filters regularly.

80. Check the weather stripping around all doors and windows.

81. Close the damper on your fireplace.

82. Close or block the foundation vents during the winter months.

83. Shut off the heat in vacant parts and rooms of your house.

84. Lower your thermostat to 68°.

Final Money-Saving Tips

85. Buy slightly damaged furniture through a wholesaler or a specializing outlet store.

86. Make tremendous savings by buying used furniture in good condition.

87. Get haircuts at a local barbers' college.

88. Have your hair dressed at a ladies' beauty college.

89. Carry adequate insurance on your personal property and belongings, but not more than you need. It is a waste of money to pay for more than your house and belongings are worth, for the simple reason that insurance companies will pay no more than what your loss is.

90. Save money by doing it yourself. Many manuals and do-it-yourself materials are available today that can aid you in doing many different types of painting, patching, mending, and other home maintenance. For example, lumber yards will cut your boards to the exact size that you ask them to, so, without being a carpenter, you can actually build your own cupboards.

91. Buy Christmas wrappings and cards after Christmas.

92. Exchange babysitting with friends.

93. Look for enjoyable forms of entertainment that are inexpensive.

94. Give yourself a home permanent.

95. Get your clothes cleaned at bulk rate.

96. Buy permanent-press clothing in order to save cleaning bills.

97. Make things last by taking good care of what you have. Make your money work for you!

GUIDELINES FOR INVESTMENTS— MAKE YOUR MONEY WORK FOR YOU

The purpose of these guidelines is not to attempt a comprehensive study of such a complex subject, but merely to point out a few helpful guidelines which will assist you in investments. For these guidelines I am indebted to my close friend, Bill Hammerbeck, who is one of the outstanding lay Christian leaders in the city of Portland and a partner in one of the well-known local investment companies.

1. Before you are ready to invest, you must first take care of your family's needs. Before any person should consider investing money, he should first provide for his own family. He will want to provide for them suitable housing, accompanied by adequate insurance. Having done this, he should then strive to build up savings reserves which are sufficient to carry him through at least six months of ill health and reverses. Before one is ready to invest, he should first have a home that he is buying, plus reserves in a savings account.

2. *Now you are ready to look at and plan your investment program.* Here you should acquaint yourself with the different investments that are available. Seek out wise counselors and learn all you can.

3. *In the investment program, it is important to keep your investments diversified.* Don't make the mistake of investing everything in either real estate or stocks, but diversify your investments into different programs. Even within a given area, such as stocks, you will want to diversify your investments further. *Whatever you do, don't put all your eggs in one basket.*

4. *Investment programs should be tailor-made to your own needs.* You'll want to consider these important questions: How old are you? What are your financial objectives? How much risk can you afford in investing? What tax benefits do you need from investing?

5. *Investigate thoroughly before you invest.* Don't suddenly jump in simply because someone has given you a hot tip. Many an investor has been led astray by a well-meaning friend's hot tip, and sometimes not even a well-meaning person's tip!

6. *Don't be too greedy.* Sometimes people try to get too much money out of a property or from a stock, holding on till the right opportunity is passed.

7. *Practice patience, the key to successful investment programs.* When the market drops, don't overreact. Hold steady, be patient, and take the long look. Give the investment the period of time that it needs to make you money.

8. Don't allow yourself to become overextended. Keep sufficient money in reserve to cover emergencies. Pay attention to your cash flow, and see to it that you have more than enough adequate cash flow to care for current expenses. Unfortunately, there are some very large companies that have been in hot water financially in recent years simply because they have overextended themselves.

9. Never speculate more money than you can afford to lose.

10. Find the kind of investment that best accomplishes your goals and objectives.

11. Don't be afraid to admit when you've made a bad investment. At some time or other everyone makes a bad investment. The wise person is the first to admit when the investment has gone sour, taking whatever action he needs to get out of it as soon as possible. *Don't follow bad money with good money.*

12. Change with the times. Don't become so committed to one type of investment that you can't be flexible and change when a greater opportunity comes in a new area of endeavor.

143